TEACHING ONLINE

EVERYTHING YOU NEED TO KNOW ABOUT ONLINE
LEARNING TO MAKE A SMOOTH, EFFORTLESS
TRANSITION

SELENA WATTS

CONTENTS

This lesson plan checklist includes:

- The 10 essential elements of a lesson plan that will help you teach with complete confidence.
- High-quality items that you can use to help you get the most from your students.
- Where you can buy these items for the lowest price.

The last thing we want is for your lessons to be less than perfect because you weren't prepared.

To receive your essential 10-point lesson planning checklist, simply scan the QR code below:

INTRODUCTION: ONLINE TEACHING, THE NEW FRONTIER

"Technology is just a tool. In terms of getting the kids to work together and motivating them, the teacher is the most important."

— (GATES)

For a lot of teachers, the mere thought of moving away from traditional methods and moving into online teaching is both overwhelming and scary.

Do you feel this way too?

If you do, you're not alone. Even I used to feel that way. These days, online teaching is very popular. But beyond that, it has also become necessary because of the state our world is in right now. At the writing of this book, we are currently in the throes of a global pandemic. If we as teachers cannot transition to online learning, the educational system will stop being effective and students will suffer as a result.

If you are reading this book, it means that you are interested in learning about online teaching. For this, you should already have confidence in your current skills and experiences as a teacher. If you feel like you need to improve yourself (to prepare for online teaching), then you should also read the first book in my series of teaching books that's entitled, *Teaching Yourself to Teach*. In the first book, you will learn all about becoming the best teacher you can be while combining traditional and online learning. Here, we will be focusing on online teaching as this has become part of our "new normal." That being said, even new teachers will be able to gain a lot of practical advice for this book.

Although the term "online learning" has become very popular now, it still seems like an alien concept to a lot of teachers, especially if you have only learned and used the traditional methods ever since you became a teacher. No matter how many years of experience you have had as a teacher, there is always room to grow, learn, and evolve. Right now, learning how to conduct your classes online is what you have to focus on.

You have a long road ahead of you. But as someone who has enormous experience with online learning, I can confidently say that this particular method of teaching is both challenging and fun. Yes, you will have to explore new ways of teaching and reaching out to your students. But as you discover these new techniques and skills, you will also find out just how much potential you have as a teacher in the modern world.

By reading this book, you will unleash a wealth of information that will help you become an innovative educator. Here, you will learn things like the benefits of online teaching, how online teaching differs from classroom teaching, the different types of online courses you can explore, the best online teaching practices, the most helpful online teaching tools, how to transition into online teaching, and so much more. By the end of this book, you will feel confident enough to create your own courses. Incidentally, that is also the third installment of my book series: "Creating Courses". If you want to continue developing your skills in this area then I do recommend reading this book, I'm sure you will enjoy it and find it very useful.

But let's go back to online teaching. By now, you must be wondering who I am and why you should continue reading. If I were in your place, I would be wondering the same thing. So, before we continue, let me share my story with you.

I am a teacher who has gone to great lengths to improve myself in different ways. When I first started teaching, I realized that I had a long way to go before I could be as confident as my co-teachers. I already considered myself a good teacher but I wanted to become one of the best. That's when I decided to learn everything I could about traditional and classroom teaching methods. After spending many years researching and testing new techniques, I was eventually able to apply everything I'd discovered until I felt like I was giving my students the best learning experiences possible.

Just as I was feeling happy and confident about my skills, online teaching emerged. As a teacher who had only relied on traditional methods, online teaching seemed like a huge challenge to me. There were new terms to learn, new methods to explore, and even new ways to communicate with students and parents! Not to mention the new paperwork that come with it. I felt like I was back to square one and it made me feel frustrated.

But I didn't let my frustrations stop me from moving forward. There wasn't time to gradually introduce online learning, so I knew there was no time to waste. My learning curve would be steep and fast.

Just as I learned how to improve myself as a teacher using traditional methods, I also learned everything I could about online teaching. Then I started making the transition into online teaching by combining it with the traditional teaching methods I was already proficient with. I applied both methods to create an amazing blended learning experience for my students—and I saw firsthand how enriching this combination can be.

I spend a lot of time exploring and testing the different strategies for online teaching. Because of my passion and dedication to teaching, I want to share everything I have learned with teachers just like you. Hence, I wrote this book. I care deeply about the benefits of online teaching to students and I believe that all teachers should try everything they can to provide their students with the best possible learning experiences. Once you accept the fact that we are now living in a digital world, it will become easier for you to be open-minded when it comes to online teaching.

Even though I believed in the traditional classroom methods (and I still do), I realized how amazingly effective online teaching is too. As you go through the different chapters of this book, you will also come to realize how you can apply what you are learning to your current teaching style. Online teaching shouldn't be a hindrance—it should be something you use to become a well-rounded, versatile teacher.

Prepare yourself to step outside of your comfort zone. Accept that you will have to start thinking out of the box. Once you have done these things, all you have to do is keep turning the pages so that you can start exploring the wonderful world of online teaching and how to become a master at it.

1

WELCOME TO THE WORLD OF ONLINE TEACHING

Online teaching is more than just a trend, it has now become a norm, especially since students are encouraged to stay at home to avoid the spread of the pandemic. Online teaching is a fairly new approach to teaching that involves the use of computers, laptops or other electronic devices, and the internet to provide learning to students of different ages and levels.

In this chapter, you will gradually explore the world of online teaching. Since this approach is relatively new, it means that there is a lot for you to learn. We will start with the basics to help you understand what online teaching entails. Then as we progress, you will learn more about online teaching—this time, with everything else that you have learned in the earlier chapters.

During your first few days, weeks, and months as a teacher, you would have gone through an adjustment period, especially if you had a lot of disruptive or challenging students in your class. Although online teaching doesn't always include face-to-face interaction, you will still have to go through an adjustment period before things start getting easier for you. The good news is you are now in the process of arming yourself with the knowledge you need to help you get through this adjustment period. Good for you!

Now, before we move forward, you should first ask yourself about your fundamental teaching philosophy. Take a moment to reflect and consider what you believe is your role as a teacher in the class. Are you the type of teacher who guides and facilitates your students' learning in class? If so, your main focus would be to help your students learn and develop their skills on their own—you are mainly there to help. Or perhaps you consider yourself a subject matter expert since you have the knowledge, and you are responsible for imparting what you know through teaching? If so, your main focus would be to teach your students using different teaching methods.

Either way, if you want to learn how to effectively teach online, then you may want to combine these approaches to make you a better teacher. By learning how to teach online, you should first rethink your teaching strategies. At some point, you will have to modify your techniques and approaches to suit the needs of your students. For instance, if you are more comfortable with being the main focus in class, this might not always be effective when you're teaching a virtual class of students from different environments. Or if you prefer facilitating activities in class, you might have to modify your methods too since you won't be able to guide your students in the same way as you do in class. Classroom management and the timing of activities are also things that I personally noticed were very different.

Yes, online teaching is a huge change. But when you reach a point where you truly understand what it entails, you will start seeing that this new method comes with its own set of unique benefits that will make your life as a teacher more fun and interesting. Overwhelming as this approach might seem right now, learning and practicing it will make things much easier for you too.

WHY CHOOSE ONLINE TEACHING?

Even before you start learning about online teaching, the first thing you might wonder is, "Why should I choose online teaching?" This is especially true if you are very good at teaching using traditional classroom methods. Since you have started teaching, you already have your own teaching style, the methods you are comfortable with, and even a number of strategies that you use to deal with challenging situations or students in your class.

The global pandemic has forced us to change our routines so instead of seeing this as a problem or a challenge that you must face, try to view it as an opportunity to improve and grow. For instance, you may have to start from square one, especially if you don't have above-average computer skills. But if you have basic knowledge on how to operate basic software or profiles on the most popular social media platforms, this may help you out. But as you will soon come to discover, there is much more to learn if you decide—or if you're required—to conduct your classes virtually.

Online teaching is a new, innovative approach to teaching that comes with a wide range of potential benefits for teachers, students, and schools. Since this book is all about online teaching, let us take a look at the advantages of this method:

Ease and Convenience

Since online teaching is primarily done online, you won't have to print out tests, handouts or quizzes. Also, you won't have to prepare materials for crafting activities or any other hands-on activities your students will do in the classroom. Instead, you will simply create or download worksheets on your computer, think of level-appropriate assignments for your students to complete at home, and give online assessments. It's that simple! Just imagine the bliss— no queueing at the photocopier!

Almost everything you will do to teach your students will be done online. The good news is that most schools provide their teachers with the materials and lesson plans. Of course, this will make things easier for you. But if you really want to become a master at online teaching, then you should also learn how to create your own lesson plans, worksheets, and materials for your students. In some cases, you might even have to modify the materials given by your school to optimize them for online use. The more you apply what you will learn in this book (and through your experiences), the simpler online teaching will be. Doing this will also help you become a well-rounded teacher.

Aside from being so simple and easy, online teaching is also very convenient. As long as you have a laptop and a reliable internet connection, you can teach your students no matter where you are in the world. This is why some schools even employ teachers from different countries—because it's possible. Not only can you increase the talent, but you also have a greater pool of experts. Students and teachers can gain from sharing language classes and immersing themselves in bilingual environments.

Time and Schedule Flexibility

These benefits apply to teachers and students alike. As a teacher, you may have the option to choose your class schedule based on your availability. Even if your school sets your class schedules for you, online classes are still more flexible than traditional school classes. After your class, you don't have to stay within the school premises and wait for the end of your shift. Instead, you can go outside to run errands, do your house chores or work on other tasks you need to accomplish.

If your students need more time to accomplish the tasks you have given them, you can give them the time they need. If you need to push your scheduled class back for a few minutes, simply inform your students about this change. You can do this by sending them a message or a short email that includes all of the details of the change. In other words, teaching online gives you the flexibility to make changes in your schedule as needed.

Location Flexibility

Just as online teaching offers flexibility in terms of timings and schedules, it also offers flexibility in terms of location. Through online teaching, you can reach out to your students at home, in school, at the office or even in a cafe. As long as you can focus on your students and provide them with the best learning experience, then you can teach wherever you are.

Of course, creating your own online teaching space at home or having one at your school will always be the best option. But if you are in a pinch and your class is coming up, it's good to know that you can simply log on using your computer, and start teaching,

A Wealth of Online Resources

Another amazing thing about online teaching is that it comes with a wealth of online resources—and most of them are free for you to access. Through information sharing, you and your co-teachers can share resources, take turns in creating activity sheets for your students to use, and even give each other new ideas for online resources to use for teaching. As you experience online teaching, you will learn more about the many resources available online and how to use them.

All over the world, there are online instructors who work for organizations that provide access to online research journals, lesson plans, academic magazines, eBooks of different topics, and even business research. Such resources have emerged for the purpose of helping teachers provide learning online. These resources are extremely valuable for teaching and for your own learning too. Some examples of these include Virtual LRC, Internet Public Library, Scholastic Teachables, and Education Resources Information Center (ERIC). Later, you will also discover some amazing online tools and resources to use for the different aspects of online teaching.

If you have any questions or concerns with issues like troubleshooting or how to deal with difficult students in a virtual classroom, for example, you can join online forums and discussions to find the answers you need. Whatever you might need to help you or improve your online teaching, you will be able to find through these resources. And you can access all of these in the comfort of your home.

Diverse and Enriching Teaching Experiences

As an online teacher, you will get the chance to teach students from all around the globe. If you are currently employed with a school that only caters to students in your state or city, that's okay. But if the management of your school decides to branch out or if you decide to apply for an online teaching job that gives you the opportunity to educate a diverse group of students, you stand to learn a lot.

If you get the chance to teach students from different countries and cultures, you will learn more about them. In the same way, your students will also get the chance to interact with other students with varied backgrounds. As I mentioned before, this type of experience is essential for language learning in real-life situations. This is a unique benefit of online teaching that doesn't come as easily as traditional classroom teaching.

Aside from this, you will also get the chance to give different types of teaching methods and strategies a try. These include teaching using presentations, screen sharing, and even using online resources like videos to engage your learners. If this is your first time teaching online, you can experiment with different methods to see which ones you are comfortable with and which ones work well for the students in your class. Just like in traditional classroom teaching, you may have to do a bit of trial-and-error to "find your groove" and start enjoying your online classes.

Immediate Feedback

By nature, online classes promote discussion and interaction. As a teacher, you can see all of your students on the screen of your computer. As you are teaching, you can immediately identify the students who seem to be struggling with your lesson, as well as the students who are actively engaged and interested in your lessons. Through this, you can provide immediate feedback by asking students if they have any questions to help them get back on track. This is more beneficial for you and your students as opposed to only discovering which students are struggling after you give an assessment in class.

Immediate feedback is also an excellent benefit for when you are giving assessments. Typically, when students take assessments online, they immediately get their score or grade a few minutes after submission. Aside from being able to see student results right away, you can even use an online grading tool that immediately gets your students' results and records them on a spreadsheet. If your school makes use of such a tool, you may have to undergo some kind of training to learn how to use it. But in the long run, this will make grading a much easier task for you.

Learning New Skills

Another benefit of teaching online is that it gives you a chance to learn new skills. Whether you have basic computer skills or you're fairly tech savvy, there is a lot for you to learn when you start teaching online. Some examples of the skills you will learn include working with different types of software, making, editing, and uploading videos, troubleshooting, and using video conferencing apps.

Going back to the many resources available for online teachers, you can find tons of tutorial videos and how-to articles where you can learn all of these skills. Make a list of the skills you need or want to learn then search for them online. After a few months or so, you will be surprised at how much you have learned and how easy the process was.

Non-Teaching Benefits

Online teaching also offers a number of non-teaching benefits. Even while at home, you can communicate with your co-teachers and the management of your school through online apps. You can have online faculty meetings, chat groups, forums, and the like to communicate with each other and discuss what needs to be done for the whole school year. Communicating online also allows you to stay updated in terms of new policies, changes in curricula or any other issues that your school might have.

The bottom line is that the online world offers endless possibilities. Now that most of us are encouraged to stay home because of the global pandemic we are facing at the time when this book was written, the best way for us to cope is by going online and continuing with our passion, which is to teach our students.

THE POSSIBLE DOWNSIDES AND RESTRICTIONS OF ONLINE TEACHING

Wonderful as online teaching is, this method isn't perfect. Just like any other teaching method, it does come with its own set of challenges and downsides. For you to understand what online teaching is all about, it's better to learn everything about it— both good and bad. So now, let's go through the various restrictions and downsides of online teaching that you must be aware of:

If you don't have the ability or access to technology

Although almost all parts of the world have access to technology, this doesn't mean that this applies to everyone. If you are an old-fashioned type of person, you might not even own a laptop or a computer to start with. In such a case, you have to find a way to obtain a computer, a laptop or a tablet for you to start teaching online. If you have no idea how to choose the best one, you may ask one of your co-teachers to help you out.

After you purchase a device, the next thing you must do is learn how to use it. Not having the knowledge, skills or ability to use technological devices is a huge hindrance in the world of online teaching. Again, you may ask one of your co-teachers to help you out. Even better, you can ask the management of your school to assign someone to give training about the basic computer skills you need to start teaching online. But if you're currently working from home and you cannot ask these people to help you, seek assistance from friends and family. In particular, reach out to the younger generation as they typically know a lot about computers. As long as you find someone who is willing to help you out, you can learn what you need.

If you're not ready to purchase a computer or laptop just yet, you can start learning the skills you need in internet cafes and shops. By going to places like these, you can learn new things and practice what you have learned without investing in a device yet. After you have learned the basic skills, then you can think about investing in a computer for your online teaching needs.

If your school doesn't provide training for you

Speaking of training, the next downside of online teaching is a lack of training by schools. Imagine how difficult it would be to teach an online class if you weren't computer literate. For you to be able to teach an online class, you need the right software, you need to know how to connect to the internet, you need to know which online apps or tools to use, and you need to know basic troubleshooting so that you can deal with issues as they arise during your online class.

If your school requires you to transition to online training but you don't know how to do it, approach your school principal or whoever is in charge of professional training programs. Ask them about the possibility of having an introductory course for you and the other teachers to know how to go about this new teaching method. Most schools will provide such training to their teachers but if you don't think it will happen at your school, you should speak up. That way, your lack of skills won't have to be a hindrance. Besides, after reading this book, you will already have a general idea of how to go about online teaching. Then all you need is to sit in front of your computer and apply what you have learned.

Be proactive about online training being provided. It's true that now, many schools are updating their systems and resources. For those who were closed down with less than a week's notice, it wouldn't have been possible to set up an intricate online learning platform. Department heads may need advice and help from teachers and you may find that if no training system is in place, you will soon have enough confidence to be the "go-to" teacher.

If your device isn't powerful enough

Even if you already own a device to use for online teaching, you have to check whether it's powerful enough to handle all of the tasks you need to perform for this teaching method. To have clear and seamless online classes, you need a user-friendly, powerful, and reliable device. If your device is too slow and it takes forever to respond to commands, you might have to delete or transfer your files to free up some memory space.

If your device keeps shutting down without warning, you should consider getting a new one. Issues like these can cause a lot of stress for you and your students. Even if you know how to troubleshoot your device, having to deal with issues like these takes time and effort. You will also lose your focus. By the time you have dealt with the issue, you might have already lost the interest of your students—or you might have run out of time. Before you start teaching online, make sure that you have a good device to work with. Invest in a good back up hard drive. Store as much data as you can on the hard drive and only have the necessary applications open. This can greatly boost performance.

If you don't have access to the internet

For most people, the internet has become a permanent part of their lives. But as popular and seemingly indispensable as the internet is, some people don't rely on it as much. Again, this negative side of online teaching might apply to you if you're not as updated in terms of the digital and online trends. You may use the internet once in a while—only when you need to—but if you plan to start teaching online, you must have a stable internet connection in your home. If you don't have one yet, you can inquire with internet providers in your locale for this. That way, not having access to the internet won't be a problem for you.

If your curriculum doesn't fit into online teaching

For you to provide your students with the best learning experience, you must make sure that your curriculum fits into virtual online learning. If you are suddenly thrust into the world of online teaching and you are in charge of a subject like Music of Physical Education, how do you teach these subjects online? This is one of the most significant downsides of online teaching.

But it doesn't have to be.

If you feel like your curriculum doesn't match this innovative teaching method, you have to find ways to change that. This is the kind of situation where you may have to completely abandon your traditional methods and develop new ways to introduce your lessons to your students in a virtual setting. You can learn more about this in the next book in my series which is all about creating online courses. For now, the best advice I can give you is to research how other teachers have found ways to fit their curricula into online teaching. Join online forums to see what other teachers have to say. Then you can do your own brainstorming session and have your ideas approved by the management of your school before you put those ideas and plans into action. P.E was a major concern for children during the strictest of lockdowns and there were some excellent trainers who created online content for students. Check out Joe Wicks in the U.K and his program PE with Joe.

If you thrive on working with other people

Finally, if you prefer working with other people, whether these are your students or co-teachers, then online teaching might feel challenging for you. Even though this method is simpler and more convenient, it can also feel quite lonely, especially if you thrive on face-to-face interactions. But you don't have to feel limited by the virtual world. Instead, find ways to make your classes more interesting. Reach out, make jokes, respond. These are some ways to help make this method a little less lonely so that you can start seeing the benefits it has to offer.

As you can see, there are ways for you to overcome the restrictions and limitations of online teaching. If any of these apply to you, then you have to work extra hard to become a successful online teacher. But in the end, all of your efforts will be worth it as you see yourself improve and you feel enjoyment while teaching your students online.

STARTING OFF WITH THE BASICS

Now that you know both sides of online teaching, it's time to start the actual learning process. To kick-start your online teaching journey, the first thing you must familiarize yourself with are the basic terms used in online teaching. This is an important step so that you will understand the definitions, explanations, and discussions about this new and innovative approach to teaching. Also, understanding these basic terms will equip you with the knowledge you need to navigate the online teaching tools that you will be using in the future.

Asynchronous Online Learning

Asynchronous online learning means that you will communicate with your students at different times throughout the day. In an asynchronous online classroom, there will be a delay in your lessons because you will communicate through emails and discussion boards. Another way to look at it is, delivering your lessons and allowing your students to participate or deliver their requirements at different times.

Typically, courses that are studied through asynchronous online learning are time-constrained, which means that you would have to complete everything within a quarter, semester or term. Here, there would be flexibility in terms of the learning materials and coursework that you provide to your students. You would make these available to your students for a specific period of time until all of them have seen or completed the material. After the deadline has passed, you can either provide new learning materials or assign homework to check if your students understood the lesson. This style of teaching offers flexibility in terms of time for you and your students.

Synchronous Online Learning

As you would assume, synchronous online learning is the opposite, where all students are learning at the same time. Although you might think of this as more suited to corporate environments and employee training, a shared online learning environment can be used in teaching too. Webinars and conferences sound a little formal, I call it our invisible classroom, the element of mystery seems to amuse the children! Chat rooms are another example.

You may have heard some horrifying stories of trying to get all students into one online learning environment and yes, it has been one of my biggest challenges, but it is also incredibly rewarding. Once you have been out of the classroom for a while, it sounds strange, but you start to miss the bustle of all the kids together, there is an element of social interaction that is very important for children in particular.

If you plan to use this method, make sure to inform your students that they have to show up at the time you have set so that they don't miss a class.

Blended Learning

Blended learning is a unique teaching method that combines online teaching with traditional methods. Although online learning is becoming more popular as a standalone approach, it first became popular as part of blended learning. Combining the traditional methods with online learning is very effective as it allows you to use the methods you are already comfortable with along with online methods that are new, innovative, and interesting. If you're interested in blended learning, you can read more about this in the first book of my teaching series, entitled, *Teaching Yourself to Teach*.

Chat Room

A chat room is an online or virtual space where you can communicate with your students in real time. While in a chat room, you can type your message and as soon as you click the "send" button, your students will receive your message instantly. In the same way, when your students send you messages in a chat room, you will be able to read them right away.

While video conferencing apps are mainly used to conduct online classes, you can use chat rooms to talk to your students about any issues, concerns or clarifications they might have with their assignments, with your lessons, or anything else related to school. Sometimes, you can also send files like handouts or activity sheets through chat rooms. And when your students have accomplished these, they can send their completed work right back to you through the chat room. Online chat is extremely useful because it's like a digital copy of your notes. Once the class has finished, you can go back through the chat and see areas for improvement or topics that need to be revised.

Computer Specifications

Computer specifications refer to the technical descriptions of the capabilities and components of your computer. Isn't that a mouthful? In simpler terms, these are the descriptions of the parts of your computer and the things that it can do. If you plan to teach online, you may need a number of computer specifications to ensure that your online classes run smoothly without interruptions. For instance, if you will teach daily online classes and you need to create or edit videos for your students, then you have to purchase a laptop or computer with the necessary specifications.

Most downloadable software programs include a list of computer specifications needed to download and operate them. If you want to check the specs of your computer, you can click on the 'Start' menu, click on the 'Control Panel', then click 'System Maintenance' or 'System'. Here, you will see the specifications of your computer including the system type, system, processor, and memory. If you're using a Mac, select the Apple menu and click "About This Mac." This will give you an overview of your device including all of its specs. If your online course requires certain specifications and you are still planning to purchase a laptop, you should make a list of the specs you need then bring that list to the shop where you plan to purchase your computer. That way, you can be sure that the device you purchase meets all of the requirements.

Usually, the most important specification you need to check is the memory. With a huge memory capacity, you can conduct online classes, download various programs, and even save your personal files on your computer. So, you should think about this when choosing a computer to purchase for your online teaching needs.

Discussion Board

Discussion boards are mainly used for the discussion of classroom materials with your students. On a discussion board, you will post questions or topics wherein all of your students would have to give their own input regarding what you have posted. Sometimes, you may require your students to discuss with each other on the discussion board while you assess their online interactions. For each class you have or each subject that you teach, you may use discussion boards in different ways. The important thing here is to make things clear for your students so that they know exactly what they are required to do.

When planning the use of discussion boards in your online classes, consider classroom etiquette too. Sometimes, students might feel like there are no rules or limitations when it comes to online classes. Since they can freely interact with each other on social media platforms, they might feel like they can do this on your discussion boards too. Before you allow your students to interact or post anything on discussion boards, make sure to set rules and guidelines first. Remind your students that the discussion board is only for school-related use. This is not the place where students should disrespect you, demean each other or discuss things that aren't related to the subject or topic that the discussion board is meant for.

You should also be very careful of your grammar when using discussion boards. As a teacher, you should make sure that everything you post is flawless. While checking what your students post or say in these discussion boards, make sure to check their grammar too. Just because discussion boards are more flexible and allow for creativity, you should still check little details like these to ensure that your students are getting the most out of the discussion boards. I probably sound like a right old lady, but I have banned all "QQFYs" and "NVMs". If they have the ability to game for hours, they have the ability to type words— and it saves me having to look them all up!

Distance Learning

Distance learning is a modality of delivering learning that is needed when teachers and students are in different locations. Distance learning isn't the same as online learning although the latter can be part of the former. In distance learning, you will provide your students with learning materials by sending them through physical mail. In some cases, you may send the materials electronically. But in online learning, you would typically use some type of Learning Management System.

Here, your students will initiate the interactions, which means that you have to follow their learning pace and structure. For distance learning, your students aren't required to follow a schedule or calendar that you have set for them. This modality has been around even before the digital age and it may have influenced the strategies that we now use for online teaching.

Flipped Classroom

In a flipped classroom, you will give your students lessons and content that they will study at home using online software and other similar tools. Then when your students are in the class-room, they will apply what they have learned. Through a flipped classroom, your face-to-face lessons become richer as your students can explore your content more, solve problems, and work together to understand the lessons.

Gamification

Gamification refers to teaching that involves games and playing mechanisms. Within the context of online teaching, it involves the use of games within your online lessons and courses for the purpose of engaging your students and encouraging interaction. Gamification is a very effective method to use, especially if you have students who are fond of playing games. When using gamification as part of your online teaching strategies, you have to find ways to make it challenging for your students. For instance, you can come up with interactive quests, challenges or board games for your students to accomplish wherein they will also learn important concepts along the way.

When you use gamification, focus on the motivation and engagement of your students. You can think of yourself as the game master and your students as the players. If you really get into it, you can have fun too! Gamification isn't meant to be a serious process. It's more about incorporating fun into your teaching strategies to help your students learn more effectively.

Hybrid Courses/Hybrid Learning

Hybrid courses and hybrid learning are similar to blended learning since they involve the combination of online teaching with face-to-face instruction. But the difference is that most of the face-to-face instruction will be replaced by online teaching. There is no standard ratio for online teaching vs. face-to-face instruction for your method to be considered as hybrid learning or a hybrid course. As long as you can provide your students with an excellent learning experience.

When it comes to hybrid learning, the best way to succeed is by integrating online and face-to-face components in a complementary way. As with other methods, one of your goals is to improve the engagement and learning of your students.

Learning Content Management System

A Learning Content Management System (LCMS) is a software you can use to develop, create, and publish content for your students. Here, you will work with your own content, which means that this type of software is ideal for those who are tech savvy and have advanced computer skills. Some examples of LCMSs today are TalentCards, eFront, and Freestone.

Learning Management System

A Learning Management System (LMS) is a software you can use to manage your blended or online teaching strategies. With an LMS, you can report, document, track, and deliver learning programs, educational courses, and other school-related materials. Some examples of LMSs today are Canvas, Google Classroom, and Blackboard Learn.

Microlearning

Microlearning involves providing your students with modular knowledge materials or short lessons for personalized and adaptive learning. Because the content you will provide to your students is short, the standout feature of this type of learning is speed. If you plan to use microlearning, make sure you can create content quickly too.

Mobile Learning

Mobile learning involves the use of e-learning resources and educational apps to teach your students. Using multi-device apps allows your students to learn with flexibility—it means that they can learn whenever and wherever they want. Just like distance learning, you will follow the pace of your students.

Online Assessment

Online assessment is a new way of assessing your students using online methods, systems, and tools. While your students are learning online, you will keep track of their progress by recording their grades or scores and giving them assessments to check how well they have understood your lessons. Through online assessments, you will gain a better understanding of your students, how they learn, and whether or not your teaching strategies are working. Online assessments also allow you to make adjustments to your teaching strategies based on the results you collect.

Syllabus

Just like in a traditional classroom, you need to use or follow a syllabus for your online classes. A syllabus contains valuable information about student expectations, your contact details, information about class assignments, the textbooks or online resources your students need, the schedules of your online classes, and even dates of examinations or assessments.

A syllabus is a necessary tool for your online teaching journey. You can use this as a guide to making your lesson plans for your online classes. As soon as you receive your class syllabus, you should print it out and keep it in your work area. That way, you can keep going back to it whenever you need to.

Virtual Classroom

A virtual classroom (VCR) is a learning environment that exists online, just like my invisible classroom. Here, you can interact with your students in real-time just as you would in a classroom. You will use a video conferencing app for this then you will teach your students in the same way as you would in a classroom.

Being aware of these terms and their meanings will make it easier for you to understand what you are reading so that you can apply it to your teaching methods. This will make your learning process smoother and more efficient.

2

CLASSROOM TEACHING VS. ONLINE TEACHING

I f you have been teaching for a couple of years now, you would already feel comfortable in front of a class of students. But when it comes to online teaching, you might feel like you're going back to the first day of your teaching career. There is some truth to this, but you don't have to look at it in a negative way. Try to go back to the first day when you walked inside a classroom. You would have felt a roller coaster of emotions.

The same thing may happen when you have your first online class. After planning your lesson, preparing everything you need, and even rehearsing your lesson, you will log on to the video conferencing app, and start teaching. Soon, you will realize that online teaching is a lot like teaching in the classroom too. Only this time, you will be interacting with your students using an online platform. In this chapter, we will focus on the similarities and differences between traditional and online teaching. We will also go through the pros and cons of each to help you paint a bigger picture of how these two methods work and how you can transition from one to the other seamlessly.

THE DIFFERENCE BETWEEN CLASSROOM TEACHING AND ONLINE TEACHING

Online teaching and traditional classroom teaching both involve presenting information to students while interacting with them in real-time. You don't have to feel too intimidated by the mere thought of teaching online. You can still use some of the strategies that you have been using in the classroom. Combine these strategies with the ones you will learn in this book and through your experiences as you start online teaching. Over time, you will find your groove as an online teacher and when this happens, you will feel more comfortable with this new method.

Before you get to that point, you should understand how online teaching differs from traditional classroom methods. Gaining an understanding of these differences will help you come up with a plan for how you will approach online teaching.

Schedule

As a teacher in a traditional school, you work for a set number of hours each day. For instance, you would have to be in school from 8:00 in the morning and you would remain in school until 4:00 in the afternoon. Even if your class is only from 8:30 in the morning to 2:00 in the afternoon, you have to remain in school to complete the eight-hour working day. This is a very common setup for teachers who work in traditional schools. If you have been a teacher for a couple of years now, you are probably used to this kind of schedule too. While you aren't in class, you can do things like prepare your lesson plans for the next week, create activity sheets to reinforce your students' learning or even check your students' assessments.

As an online teacher, you won't have to stick with such a rigid schedule. In fact, you might not even be required to come to school unless you absolutely need to be there. As long as you can conduct your online classes as scheduled and you can address the needs of your students and their parents, you can work with a flexible schedule. You can create your own schedule wherein you will combine online classes, communications through email or in chat rooms or through discussion boards. Of course, if your school has its own rules regarding class schedules, you have to follow these too. For instance, if you are required to conduct classes in the morning, then you have to make yourself available at that time.

Teacher Requirements

Whether you are an online teacher or a traditional classroom teacher, you must possess certain credentials to be allowed to teach. For instance, you should have taken—and passed—the international standard TESOL/TEFL requirement to be able to teach English as a Second Language whether online or offline. As a traditional classroom teacher, the other requirements would vary depending on where you are teaching. Most of the time though, you should at least have some years of teaching experience or a bachelor's degree in education. If you are already teaching at a school, it means that you possess everything they require in their teachers.

If you're planning to transition to online teaching, you may consider taking a certified program or course that focuses on online teaching. Unless your school is requiring you to transition to online teaching, taking this certification will make it easier for you to apply for online teaching jobs at different schools or as a freelancer. Because of the current situation our world is in right now, there are many opportunities for online teachers. In the US, you can take these certified programs and courses for online teaching at Johns Hopkins University (Baltimore, MD), University of Southern California (Los Angeles, CA), Columbia University (New York, NY), and University of Florida (Gainesville, FL). You may inquire at your state's local school too. It all depends on which school you want to earn your Online Teaching certifications in and if you are interested in specific courses.

Curriculum and Syllabus

Before you can start teaching online, you need a curriculum to guide you. Traditional schools already have their own curricula and syllabi that they give to their teachers at the beginning of the school year. While you may use the same files for teaching your students online, you have to check whether the lessons on your school's curricula and syllabi can be taught online.

If not, then you will need to prepare a new curriculum and a new syllabus to follow, or at least tweek the old work so that it functions with online teaching. Naturally, this entails more effort on your part. But if you can create these specifically for your online class, it will become easier for you to teach. In the beginning, this might be challenging for you. But you can always use your traditional curriculum and syllabus to guide you as you create new ones.

Teaching Environment

This is a given really! This is the biggest difference between traditional classroom teaching and online teaching. Traditional teaching is done in a classroom where you interact with your students face to face. You will conduct your lessons and activities in the classroom and both you and your students would have to be physically present in class every day. Online teaching, on the other hand, only occurs in a virtual classroom.

For this, you need a laptop or a computer, a reliable connection to the internet, and a quiet place for you to conduct your classes. If you plan to work from home, you have to make sure that the environment where you teach will allow you to focus on your classes and on your students. There shouldn't be anything that might distract you or your students from your lessons.

Classroom Management

When you are teaching in the classroom, you can move around freely as you interact with your students. Your students can also interact with each other and work in groups if you assign such an activity. You can arrange your students in the class to make the most out of the space you have. You can also group your students who have the same learning styles so that they can help each other out.

When teaching an online class, you don't have to worry about these things. Online classes happen in a video conferencing app and all you have to do is show up. After setting the time, you will log on, initiate the group meeting, and when all of your students have joined in, you start teaching. Because of this, it's recommended to only have a few students in your online class. That way, you can still focus on them individually while you are teaching. Nevertheless, at some point in your career, you may be faced with an online class of 30 or more students, if the opportunity arises, take it. Any experience where you can learn will make you a better teacher.

Facilitation of Class Discussions

When teaching in a classroom, you can use different methods and strategies. You can stand up in front of the class and present your lesson as if giving a seminar. You can divide your students into groups and give them topics to discuss then ask them to report after a set amount of time. You can even introduce your lessons using visual aids and online tools if you're using the blended learning method.

As an online teacher, you also have the option to present your lessons in different ways. You can conduct an online class and present your lesson from where you are. You can use discussion boards to initiate discussions between yourself and your students. You can also ask your students open-ended questions then give them a chance to share their thoughts. Just make sure that the activities you plan are engaging and interesting so that your students will listen and participate throughout your lessons instead of getting distracted by things in their homes.

Learning Outcomes

As a teacher in a traditional classroom, it's easy to identify what your students must learn and be able to do by the end of your course. If you are employed by a school, you would already have a list of learning outcomes that you use as the basis of your lessons. This means that you won't have to list these learning outcomes because they would already be available.

But if you plan to teach online, you have to learn all about learning outcomes and teaching techniques that are specific to virtual learning. If your school has required you to teach online for whatever reason, then they might provide these resources for you. However, you may have to learn how to come up with learning outcomes on your own. You can base these on the learning outcomes of your traditional classroom but this time, consider the other differences and the limitations of online teaching.

Completion of Assignments and Grading

In the classroom, you can assign work to your students that they will accomplish in the class. Once in a while, you can give them homework to complete then submit in school the next day. You will assign grades to all of the activities that your students complete, both in school and at home. Depending on the requirements of your school, you can record your students' grades in a grading book or on a spreadsheet that you update on your computer.

As an online teacher, you can only assign work for your students to accomplish at home. After all, they will be studying from home. Therefore, it becomes more difficult to gauge the skills of your students as you won't know if they accomplished their work independently or if their parents helped them out. Either way, you have to come up with a system for grading their work. Speaking of grades, you can use an LMS to record your students' grades. This is easier and more convenient, especially if you know how to automate the process.

As you can see, traditional teaching is very different from online teaching. But now that you know what makes them different, you can understand both methods better. Whether you plan to start with blended learning first or you want to transition to online teaching right away, you first need to come up with a plan for how to make the change.

THE PROS AND CONS OF CLASSROOM TEACHING

At this moment, how long have you been a classroom teacher?

When I wrote this book, I had already been teaching in a classroom for years. I was comfortable with it, I enjoyed it, and teaching in front of a class reinforced my belief that teaching was my calling. Traditional classroom teaching occurs inside a classroom. You and your students would come to class each day so that you can teach and they can learn. It's simple, retro, and extremely effective. For most teachers, their first teaching experience would have been in the classroom. Until now, many teachers from all over the world prefer classroom teaching to online teaching as it has a number of advantages over the modern, virtual method:

- If you are employed at a school, you won't have to find

students to teach on your own. The management of your school will deal with marketing, enrollments, and assigning students in the different classes. Once you are assigned to a class of students, you can start teaching.

- Also, if you are employed at a school, you can rely on receiving a regular salary each month. Sometimes, you may even get bonuses as required by the law or if your school gives monetary rewards as part of its incentive program. Some schools even offer additional benefits like retirement plans and health insurance.

- You can teach classes within the "normal working hours" and if you are employed by a good school, you may get a lot of support along with opportunities to grow professionally.

- While teaching in a classroom, you have access to all of the facilities in your school. This means that you can employ more teaching methods to engage your students and enrich their learning experiences.

- Teaching in a classroom is a lot of fun as you don't have to just teach. I just love the atmosphere you can create on a classroom. v You can think of various activities for your students to do while in class.

- In a classroom, you have space to give your students fun activities like group discussions, role-play activities, games, debates, and even experiments.

- You get the chance to work and interact with a class

face to face. This allows you to plan interactive and dynamic lessons that will make your teaching experiences more rewarding, especially if you're able to execute your plans flawlessly.

- If you have students in your class who are from different countries, it is easier to learn more about their culture since you will get the chance to observe them in person. This is a wonderful learning experience for you. Having such students also gives you plenty of opportunities for "teachable moments" in your class.

- You can always ask help from your co-teachers if you need to in the middle of your lessons. For instance, if you have to make an urgent call while teaching, you can ask one of your colleagues to take over for a couple of minutes.

- You get to socialize with your students, other teachers, and the rest of the school staff. This is one of the most important advantages of traditional classroom teaching over online teaching.

As you can see, old-fashioned as classroom teaching might be, it comes with wonderful advantages. But this method isn't perfect, especially when you compare it with online teaching. Now, let's take a look at the disadvantages of classroom teaching that you may realize once you have started teaching online:

- If your salary doesn't cover all of your daily expenses, this is one disadvantage. Even though you get a regular salary, if it's not enough, you will end up struggling.
- As a classroom teacher, you have more work to deal with, especially if you plan many interactive activities in your class. As an online teacher, the bulk of your work would be lesson planning, giving homework and assessments, and teaching. But when you are a classroom teacher, you have to plan lessons, prepare materials, give assessments, check your students' work, and manage your class. If you have a lot of disruptive students, you have to work hard to manage them if you want your students to get the most out of the lessons you have planned.
- Often, classroom teachers take their work home with them. Considering the workload you have to deal with, you might not have enough time to do all of your tasks in school. Because of this, you may have to take some of your work home—such as preparing materials or grading homework—and this can be very stressful- and heavy if you use textbooks!
- Compared to online classes, classrooms typically contain many students. These large classroom sizes can be a disadvantage, especially if you have a lot of disruptive students in your class. Conversely, online classes typically consist of only a few students. This

means that it is more difficult to focus on individual students when teaching in a classroom.

- Classroom teaching isn't as flexible as online teaching, especially in terms of schedules and locations. As a classroom teacher, you have to physically go to school every day to teach your students. You also have to follow the schedule set by the school. These are huge disadvantages, especially if you prefer working from home and if you want to work with flexible hours.

Classroom teaching has its own pros and cons. But if you have been a classroom teacher for a long time now, you should have already found ways to overcome these challenges. One thing's for sure: Classroom teaching is much more rewarding since you get to observe your students and interact with them face to face. This is a very important benefit for you and your students.

But since we all have to keep up with the times, you also have to learn online teaching. If you have the opportunity, you may want to start with blended learning as this will make your transition into online learning much easier. Blended learning involves both online and classroom teaching, so it has the potential to make you a better teacher while providing your students with varied learning experiences.

THE PROS AND CONS OF ONLINE TEACHING

Since this book is mainly about online teaching, it aims to tell you everything about this innovative approach. You have just read all of the pros and cons of classroom teaching. If you have experienced being a classroom teacher, then you may already know these things. Online teaching, on the other hand, is something new to a lot of teachers, maybe even to you. As you embark on a journey towards becoming an online teacher, you can expect these advantages over being a classroom teacher:

- Flexibility in terms of when and where you teach. You can teach from your house, from a cafe, from your school or from anywhere else. You can also teach at your most convenient time unless you are still employed by a school and they have set a schedule for you to follow.
- Online teaching also offers flexibility in terms of attire. As a classroom teacher, you must go to school wearing something that looks professional or even a uniform. As an online teacher, you can wear casual clothing that allows you to teach comfortably.
- Since online teaching is very popular these days, employers offer good rates to teachers who want to teach online. If you can prove that you are an excellent teacher, you have the potential to earn good money while working from home.

- As an online teacher, you have the option to take on as many students or classes as you can handle. Even if you only have a single class each day, you have the option to take on other projects and freelance work so that you can earn enough to support yourself and your family.
- You have 24/7 access to all of the teaching materials that your employer provides. You also have the option to access the countless educational resources available online.
- If you are following standardized coursework, you don't even have to create lesson plans. You simply follow what is given to you.
- Becoming a teacher in a school that focuses only on online learning allows you to teach students from different parts of the world. This is a wonderful way for you to meet new people from across the globe in the comfort of your home.
- As an online teacher, you won't be "responsible" for your class. Since your students will be in their own homes, all you have to do is teach them. You don't have to worry about their safety, you don't have to worry about your students getting into fights, and you don't have to deal with highly disruptive students. Even if you have such students in your class, it's much easier to deal with them because you can just mute

their audio so that they won't disturb the other students.

- Online teaching allows you to conduct one-on-one classes. Such classes allow you to check the comprehension of your students as you don't have to focus on other students while teaching.
- In some cases, online teaching doesn't involve giving quizzes, seat work, tests or even grades. After teaching, you would simply give an assessment to your students that is scored and recorded by an LMS. So easy!
- Finally, online teaching isn't as exhausting as classroom teaching. Handling a virtual class doesn't involve a lot of physical activity, which means that you won't feel tired at the end of the day. Of course, you should also get up and move once in a while because sitting in front of the computer all day isn't good for your health.

The advantages of online teaching over classroom teaching are evident. Still, if you are used to teaching in a class, you might not see the value of these advantages. But once you start teaching online, you will realize how easy and convenient it can be. However, just like classroom teaching, online teaching comes with its own set of cons such as:

- Online teaching doesn't offer the same stability as

classroom teaching. This is especially true if your salary depends on the number of classes you are able to conduct within a given period. As a classroom teacher, you can rely on a monthly salary plus benefits. But as an online teacher, you might not get paid a consistent amount each time.

- The teaching methods that you can use as an online teacher aren't as many as the ones you can use as a classroom teacher. You mainly have to rely on visual and audio methods to teach your students. This is a huge disadvantage, especially if you have students who learn better through hands-on experiences and physical movement.

- After the novelty of online teaching wears off, it can get quite lonely. If you are the type of person who thrives while working with other people, whether they be students or co-teachers, online teaching might make you feel isolated.

- If you push yourself too hard by taking on too many classes a day, there is a very high likelihood of getting burned out. Since online teaching isn't as varied and interactive as classroom teaching, you might get tired of doing the same thing over and over again. For instance, if you teach the same subject from 8:00 in the morning to 8:00 in the evening just to make sure that you're earning enough, you might get burned out after just a week or two of teaching!

- You need to make sure that your devices are always

working optimally at all times. Otherwise, you might lose students if your internet connection keeps getting cut off or if your computer keeps freezing. If you teach several online classes, it would be better to invest in a second device for you to use as a backup in case your computer fails. This can be very frustrating and expensive.

Most of the disadvantages of online teaching come from the fact that it is still new and it lacks stability. As time goes by, online teaching might become the norm but for now, we are still in the adjustment period. Nevertheless, online teaching is a wonderful approach if you can use it the right way. The good news is, you are already reading this book so you are on your way to doing just that!

SO... WHICH ONE IS BETTER?

All teachers who learn about classroom teaching and online teaching are bound to ask this question. As your mind swims with the knowledge of the pros and cons of both approaches, you will start to wonder—which one is better? When it comes to the quality of teaching, does classroom teaching rule or is online teaching the better option?

As someone who has learned, experienced, and used both methods, I don't have a definite answer for you. If you had asked me this question before I tried online teaching, I would have immediately told you that classroom teaching is the best. However, since I have also learned how to become an online teacher, I can tell you that both approaches offer something unique. They both provide you and your students with their own benefits.

At the end of the day, the answer to this question will depend on you. Let me give you some examples to illustrate this fact. If you have been a classroom teacher for years and you have already perfected your teaching style, you may end up struggling with online teaching. Even if you learn how to teach online, you might still have a strong preference for teaching in the classroom. This doesn't mean that you can't become an effective online teacher. It just means that traditional classroom teaching is more your style. But the mere fact that you are willing to learn about online teaching already says a lot about you as a teacher. If you feel like classroom teaching is still the more effective approach, then you may opt to incorporate the best online teaching strategies to improve your teaching methods and make them more modern.

But if the thought of online teaching makes you feel excited, then this approach might be the better one for you. Going back to the pros of online teaching, if you prefer flexibility and you don't mind teaching at different times of the day, then you will probably excel at teaching online. Still, you shouldn't dismiss traditional teaching methods altogether. Just as classroom teachers should employ online teaching strategies to improve their teaching methods, you can also use traditional methods to make your online teaching more interesting.

If you have to learn online teaching as part of your school's requirements, approach this task with enthusiasm and vigor. Online teaching has the potential to be very effective as long as you know how to conduct it. Start by learning the basics and the technical aspects of online teaching. This will prepare you for it. Once you get the chance to teach online, then you can start using different strategies and your own creativity to make things more engaging for your students and more fun for you too. You don't have to use these approaches exclusively. Explore different options to find what works for you and your students. As time goes by, you can continue refining your methods until you feel comfortable and confident whether you are in a physical classroom or a virtual one.

3

THE DIFFERENT TYPES OF ONLINE COURSES

Simply learning about online teaching is already a lot! But we're just getting started. By now, you're already getting a better idea of what online teaching entails and how it differs from classroom teaching. When I reached this point, I felt more excited about this innovative method—and I hope excitement is growing inside you too.

In this chapter, we will discuss the most common types of online teaching courses. No matter what age group you are handling, you can learn a lot from these courses. As a new online teacher, you will have to come up with your own plan for how you will conduct your online classes. While you will have to follow the rules set by your school or company, you also have to come up with your own strategies to make things easier and more interesting for you.

As you learn about these online courses, you will understand the different kinds of situations that may arise while teaching online. You will also have a better idea of what happens in an online classroom depending on the type of online course you are handling. Everything you will learn in this chapter will be beneficial for you, especially when you start transitioning to online teaching. If you plan to pursue a career in online teaching, this chapter will be even more beneficial for you as you will already have an idea of what to expect when you are required to teach various online courses.

Before we begin, let me first refresh your memory of blended learning/teaching. If you can recall, blended learning is a method that involves both classroom teaching and online teaching. As you go through the different courses in this chapter, you will notice that some of them involve blended learning. This is because blended learning is like combining the best of both worlds. This is something for you to consider as you go through this chapter.

Also, as you learn about the different online courses, you may want to have a pen and paper next to you. That way, you can write down all of the most interesting concepts or strategies of the individual courses. By the end of this chapter, go through the list you have made. Everything you have written down can be part of the plan you make to start your online journey. Another strategy is to highlight the interesting concepts or strategies you see for the same purpose. Either way, this chapter will help kick-start your online teaching journey as it provides lots of practical and effective strategies you can use as an online teacher.

ADAPTIVE ONLINE COURSES

Adaptive online courses are innovative. These courses are considered a type of e-learning wherein you will adapt the learning materials you use for each of your students. If needed, you will design these learning materials to ensure that each student learns what they need to at the end of the course. When conducting adaptive online courses, you would take several parameters into consideration such as the student's characteristics, skills, abilities, performance, and goals. This course allows you to focus on individualizing your students' learning, which means that it is student centered or student based.

The design of adaptive courses is meant to present these courses in a customizable and personalized way. This makes it the perfect choice if you want your individual students to get the best learning experiences possible. As the name implies, an adaptive course is built on an adaptive platform. Within this platform, you will find the learning activities and materials you need. Here, you will also find formative assessments that you can use for various learning units.

As you teach your students in an adaptive online course, you have to be very observant. You should be able to see how your students learn so that you can help them progress appropriately. When you gauge the learning level of your students, you can direct them to the best type of content for the level they are currently in. Even if you have several students enrolled in the course, they won't be progressing in the same way or time. Some of your students will get the chance to move forward with the lessons while you would have to give reinforcements to others. This means that throughout the course, you must constantly observe your students to learn about their performance, behavior, and comprehension. As they progress, you will provide them with the guidance they need to achieve the learning goals of their chosen course.

Right now, you can also use laboratory-based instructional techniques for your adaptive online courses, especially for sequencing student data mathematically. While this is one of the newer aspects of adaptive online courses, learning all about it early will give you an edge when these techniques go mainstream. Although you might find these techniques a bit challenging, they have the potential to be both effective and valuable in your online teaching career.

In this type of online course, you can utilize some type of grading software to automate the grading process. This means that after your students take their formative assessments, these will be graded automatically by measuring how well your students have understood the lessons.

When it comes to subjects or topics, the best ones that will fit into adaptive online courses are the ones that require the students to demonstrate certain skills or build their own knowledge base. The subjects should have measurable objectives for them to fit into adaptive courses. If you can create individual lessons and formative assessments for certain subjects, you can teach these in adaptive courses too. However, subjects or topics that are more subjective might not be a good fit for this type of online course. For instance, if you have to assign research projects, portfolios, reaction papers, and similar tasks to your students, you cannot use an automatic grading software to check them.

ASYNCHRONOUS ONLINE COURSES

Asynchronous online courses involve teaching students who come from different locations at different times. In other words, your classes won't occur in real time. As a teacher of an asynchronous online course, you may have students who come from different countries, which means that they have different time zones. Even if your students come from the same country as you, they might still choose to have their class at a different time than the other students. For such a course, the biggest adjustment you have to make is your schedule.

In this type of online course, you will provide your students with lessons, topics or units that they will have to learn according to their own schedules. You may use discussion boards, assign readings, upload media, give online assessments, and other activities that will help your students learn the lessons within the course. You will make these things available for your students to access whenever they go online. As the teacher, you will guide your students, provide feedback on their work, and assess their performance regularly.

As you think about the activities or lessons that you will give to your students, you should also think about how much time you will give everyone to either learn the lessons or accomplish the activities. Consider the time differences, your students' individual schedules, and their current level. Once in a while, you may get opportunities to interact with your students in real time but for these opportunities, you would have to schedule them. This type of online course is perfect for students who have busy schedules or those who are frequently under time constraints. As a teacher, you will have to make adjustments, especially if you want to schedule real-time interaction with them.

If you are thinking about teaching an asynchronous online class, you should learn everything that you can about it first. Now that you know the basic concept of how such courses work, you should be able to determine if this type of online course is right for you. To help make your choice easier, you should know the main pros and cons of asynchronous online courses. For this type of online course, the main advantages include flexibility (both for you and your students) and allowing your students to learn at their own pace—a benefit that is student centered.

However, since this online course doesn't involve real-time interaction, there is a risk that either you or your students will become apathetic towards the course. In the beginning, your students might feel empowered by self-guided learning. But after a while, they might lose interest, especially if they are used to traditional classroom learning. On your side as a teacher, you might feel isolated when all of the courses you teach are asynchronous. Although planning lessons and coming up with new material will keep you busy, not being able to communicate or interact with your students directly (or with your entire class at the same time), can eventually make you feel lonely. Consider these pros and cons if you are given the chance to pick which type of online course you will teach.

FACE-TO-FACE ONLINE COURSES

Face-to-face online courses don't offer as much flexibility as the other types since they are a lot like real-world classroom courses. Instead of giving your students the chance to learn at their own pace and their preferred time, you will conduct "face-to-face" classes in an online campus or a virtual classroom, synchronous! This type of online course allows you to use blended learning/teaching because you will be conducting classes in real time.

This type of online course is perfect for teachers like you who are new to online teaching or who are interested in transitioning to teaching online. Since these courses will be conducted in a way that's similar to the classroom setting, you might find it easier to adjust. Also, you may get the chance to employ traditional teaching methods while conducting your classes virtually. As with all the other types of online courses, you can teach students from all over the world. But unlike asynchronous courses, your students will adjust to the schedule you set for the face-to-face classes. Also, unlike traditional classes, you don't have to conduct virtual classes all day, every day.

Instead, you will simply set one face-to-face class with your students wherein all of them are required to attend no matter where they are in the world. If you have students who cannot attend your face-to-face classes (for whatever reason), you can record the session for them so they can watch it during their free time. The great thing about having a face-to-face, real-time session is that you and your students can interact with each other. During these classes, you can introduce lessons, reinforce concepts, and initiate discussions for you to see how well your students have learned and understood the lessons.

Another advantage of this type of online course is that you can also schedule one-on-one classes with your students. Apart from the virtual classes that all of your students attend, you can schedule these one-on-one sessions with each of them for a more intimate face-to-face interaction. The great thing about these individual sessions is that you can allow your students to choose the time to make sure that they will show up. Use these sessions to get a better idea of how your students are performing, how well they have understood the lessons, and for the purpose of assessment.

When teaching a face-to-face online course, the first thing you must do is share your expectations and set the rules. Just because you will be teaching in a virtual classroom, this doesn't mean that your students can do whatever they want. The rules you set will help you make sure that your online classes that only happen once a day are never wasted. Explain the rules very clearly, as well as any consequences of breaking these rules. Do this during your first face-to-face session and keep reinforcing the rules for a couple of days before you focus solely on academics. Don't forget the benefits of positive reinforcement for synchronous online teaching. Software like ClassDojo is great because you can reward children and parents can see it too.

Another thing you must focus on when teaching this type of online course is inclusion. You must make sure that all of your students interact during your classes. As much as possible, think of ways to engage each student so that everyone gets the most out of your course.

FLIPPED ONLINE COURSES

A flipped classroom involves introducing lessons and course materials outside the class. When the students enter the classroom, you will answer their inquiries, challenge them to apply what they have learned, and assess how well they have learned the lessons from the materials you have provided. The course materials you provide may include research assignments, video recordings, readings, and other materials that students learn on their own.

Although this works well for a traditional classroom, how do you conduct a flipped online course?

This is another type of online course where you can use blended learning. In fact, if you don't have a curriculum yet, you can design your curriculum to suit a flipped online course. For this, you will provide course materials to your students online giving them the chance to learn on their own. Then you will set a schedule to "meet" your students online to discuss, reflect on, and expand on what they have learned. If you want to practice teaching an online flipped course, follow these steps:

- **Plan** your lessons accordingly. Although you may use the materials your school has provided, you should also come up with your own plan for how to flip your online class. Come up with a simple lesson plan that includes an outline of the learning outcomes you expect.

- **Create** the materials to give to your students. For instance, you can record yourself introducing the lesson or come up with a video recording of your lesson that includes different elements. For instance, if you are introducing different types of artistic styles, you can create a video slideshow that includes text (to introduce the different styles) and images of samples. You can also come up with a list of links or resources that are related to the lesson.

- **Distribute** the materials that you have made. But before you do this, go through all of the materials one more time to make sure they are age and level appropriate. Also, provide your students with a list of instructions for how to use the materials along with the list of learning outcomes you have made. Finally, inform your students that it is their responsibility to learn the lessons on their own and when it's time for your online class, you will be discussing everything they have learned.

- **Discuss** the lesson in class. Ask your students to share what they have learned from the materials you gave them. As an online teacher, you will be facilitating the discussion so you should try to make it fun and engaging.

For the next lesson, just repeat these steps. It's that simple. Apart from these steps, you can make things more interesting for your students by encouraging active learning where you give your students the opportunity to apply what they have learned by sharing their experiences of giving examples.

Other great strategies include collaborative learning where you will allow your students to interact with each other in groups, debates or discussions that will surely spark interesting interactions, peer instruction where you will encourage your students to take turns in facilitating the class, and problem-solving where you will give your students problems to solve for the purpose of checking how well they have learned and understood the materials you gave them.

HYBRID ONLINE COURSES

A hybrid online course is also known as a blended online course as it combines strategies from the face-to-face course and the flipped course to create a unique and interesting combination. Although you may also incorporate traditional classroom methods here, not all of these methods will work. Instead, you may want to focus on the interactions you have with your students, as well as help them deal with any issues they have with their learning.

This type of online course also involves meeting your students in person a couple of times during the semester. Naturally, this means that you cannot have students who come from remote places as they won't be able to join your physical classes. When having physical classes, these are the best times for you to use your traditional classroom methods. Let's break down a typical hybrid course to help you understand it better:

- **Online (flipped) learning** involves giving your students materials to introduce lessons and concepts. This aspect allows your students to learn things on their own and at their own pace.
- **Face-to-face learning** involves conducting online classes in a virtual classroom. For these sessions, you would set a schedule for your students to show up. As much as possible, all of your students should be present for these online sessions.
- **Classroom learning** involves meeting in person to have classes, interact with each other, and conduct activities like role-playing, group discussions or even activities that include physical movements.

Although hybrid courses are very interesting, fun, and engaging, it will take a lot of effort from you as a teacher. You would have to plan for all of the aspects of this online course. You have to prepare all of the materials to distribute to your students for them to learn the lessons. Then you have to prepare the lessons, discussions or activities you will do for your virtual face-to-face classes. Finally, you also have to plan the activities for the physical classes you will conduct in the classroom.

Even though you will have to work harder to successfully teach a hybrid online course, you will also experience the most rewards. Here, you can use different teaching styles to help your students learn. By doing this, you can cater to the different types of learners in your class. Naturally, this ensures that they will have the best learning experiences with you as their teacher.

INDIVIDUAL AND COLLABORATIVE ONLINE COURSES

Individual learning in the context of online learning courses means that several students will be participating but they will independently work to achieve their learning goals. Here, you may teach the class and provide the same learning materials to all of the students but your students will study on their own until they reach the course's learning goals. Because of the nature of this type of online course, it isn't ideal for students who enjoy teamwork or those who want to develop their communication skills.

For students to succeed in such a course, they should possess persistence, basic technical skills, and adequate communication skills too. Since you are not expected to help your students hone these skills, they should already possess them so they don't run into any issues. Students in online individual courses should also know how to manage their time effectively as they are expected to attain the learning goals on their own. For this type of online course, your main role as a teacher is to provide learning materials and lessons, guide your students when they need help, assess your students, and monitor their progress.

At the beginning of the course, you must emphasize the independent learning aspect along with your role as the teacher. Try to explain things in a way that will keep your students motivated even if they will be learning on their own. If you want to help your students, you can even give them tips on how to optimize their learning environment at home. For instance, you can give them tips like setting up a study area in their home that is free of distractions, turning off their cellphones while they are studying and avoiding the lure of social media on their computers. Although giving such tips isn't exactly part of your responsibilities, helping your students out may motivate them more.

Collaborative online courses are another modern type of course and these are the exact opposite of independent online courses. Here, several students will learn together and try to achieve the learning goals together too. For your students to achieve their learning goals, they have to work together—or collaborate. As a teacher, you will conduct this type of online course by forming groups within your online class. The number of groups and members will depend on the number of students you have in your class. Naturally, if your online class only consists of five or six students, you can already consider them as a group without having to divide them further. If the planned activity is suitable, you could divide smaller groups into two as this creates a more competitive environment and can help engage students.

As the name implies, collaborative online courses are all about teamwork and communication. The main idea behind this online course is that knowledge develops effectively when it occurs within a group of individuals who learn from and interact with each other. Although this type of online course is more common in traditional classrooms, you can also apply it online using the right strategies and methods. For instance, this is where you can have chat rooms, discussion boards, and other communication tools. Find out which ones work best and include these in the instructions or guidelines you give to your students at the beginning of the course. You should also come up with different types of group activities that will encourage your students to have fun interacting with each other and working together.

INTERACTIVE ONLINE COURSES

Interactive online courses involve two-way interaction between you and your students. This means that you will not just be the focus of your virtual classroom. Instead, you will be communicating and interacting with your students—while they will also communicate and interact with you. This type of online course can potentially be fun and engaging, especially if your students feel comfortable enough to interact with you. For interactive online courses, there are different levels you (and your students) can choose from:

- **Full interactive learning** wherein your students must communicate and interact with you and all of the learning materials you provide. For instance, after going through or using one of the materials you have provided, they will give you feedback about it. Some examples of learning materials for this level include simulations, customized videos, interactive games, and the use of avatars.

- **Moderate interactive learning** wherein your students have more control over their online learning experiences. This level is more complex as your students can customize their activities. Since the materials you provide will be more complex too, there is a higher likelihood that your students will communicate and interact with you more frequently. Some examples of learning materials for this level include simulations, animated videos, and multimedia presentations.

- **Limited interactive learning** wherein your students are required to interact with you at least once in a while. For this level, you would also provide learning materials that require your students to interact such as multimedia presentations, drag-and-drop interactions, and clickable menus, for example.

- **Passive interactive learning** wherein your students aren't required to interact with you. Although they can communicate with you if they want, you won't expect them to as you conduct your classes. Instead, you will focus more on providing materials like videos, assessments, and online handouts, for example.

Interactive online courses are highly beneficial for teachers and students alike. Because these courses involve interaction, this makes them far more interesting than courses that involve independent learning. Therefore, if you thrive on socialization and you enjoy interacting with people, then this might be one of the best types of online courses for you.

However, the activities and learning materials you provide in interactive online courses are significantly more complex than the ones you provide to students in the other types of online courses. This is because your students would also have to interact with the materials (at different levels) too. If you are interested in teaching this type of online course, you may have to undergo training to learn how to make such materials. If your school doesn't provide such training or if you are a freelance online teacher, then you have to learn this on your own. Either way, learning how to make interactive materials will help you become a more skilled teacher no matter what type of online course you will teach.

INTRODUCTORY ONLINE COURSES

Introductory online courses are simple courses that students take if they want to pursue a more complex degree or field of study in the future. As a teacher of an online introductory course, you will provide your students with the fundamental knowledge they need for the next steps they will take. Typically, introductory courses are a prerequisite to other courses, which means that students are required to take them.

Another way to look at an introductory course is a quick preview of a course that students want to take in the future. By nature, these courses are quick, fairly simple, and as a teacher, you would only be teaching basic information. In an introductory online course, you can have short, one-on-one live sessions, live group sessions or webinars. In some cases, you can even record the sessions you conduct and offer these to students since the information that you share isn't that complex. If your students have any questions about the recorded lesson, they can simply send you a message.

As an online teacher, one of the biggest advantages of introductory courses is their simplicity. Typically, the whole course doesn't involve a lot of content either, which means that you can teach more classes. Since you don't have to prepare a lot of materials or brush up on the lessons you will teach, you can focus on scheduling more classes throughout the day. If you are a freelance online teacher, this can be very lucrative for you.

Boredom might be your biggest enemy here, especially if you have to teach the same things over and over again.

To avoid this, you may consider offering different introductory courses to different students. As long as you have the knowledge, experience, and qualifications to teach different introductory courses, you can make this type of online course work for you. The bottom line is that if you're able to design a solid introductory course, you will find success as an online teacher.

MASSIVE OPEN ONLINE COURSES

Massive Open Online Courses (MOOCs) are the best type of online course for when you have a large group of students. If you have ever tried teaching in a university in a massive classroom filled with students, this is the online version. If you are a university teacher, it might be very easy for you to transition into a MOOC. Since MOOCs are similar to traditional university classrooms, all you have to do is learn how to use your computer to conduct your classes in a virtual setting. Fortunately, there are online platforms available that you can use to conduct your course with as many as 50 students at a time.

One of the main features of a MOOC that makes it appealing to students is that it is open to everyone. As long as a student has a laptop, a stable internet connection, and the motivation to learn, they can sign up for this online course. If you are conducting this type of online course, you have the option to either limit the number of students who can join, or you can accept as many students as possible. Another feature that makes MOOCs popular with students is that usually, these courses come free of charge. Even if some schools or companies that offer MOOCs charge a fee, this fee is typically minimum so that the students can get a certificate or some other perk.

For you and your students, the best advantage of a MOOC is the flexibility in terms of the course structure. Since virtually any student can sign up for this online course, the learning is usually self-paced. Although you will conduct online classes, the students who attend would be responsible for learning at their own pace. However, for students who have enrolled in a MOOC for the purpose of obtaining academic credit or a certificate of completion, you would have to provide a structure for the course, a schedule for your students to follow, and a grading system for when you give assessments.

Probably the most significant downside of this type of online course right now is that a lot of MOOC courses aren't accredited. This means that your students won't be able to use the credits they earned from these courses when applying to universities. At the very least, your students would have learned something new through MOOCs. But as a teacher, you may want to ask the company or school you are applying for if the MOOCs they offer are accredited—and if so, at which universities. That way, you can inform your students about this or you can answer their questions if they ask.

ONLINE CERTIFICATION COURSES

Certification online courses are typically short, and they focus on a single specialization. I am a huge fan of these and actually do one a year whether it's teaching related or just something that interests me. Because of this, students who are interested in online certification courses should go through the list of programs offered along with the length of the course, and the format. The students you will have in this type of online course won't necessarily hold an undergraduate degree. Most of them would be interested in taking such a course so that they can apply for a job. If you teach this type of online course, you must possess expert-level knowledge of what you will be teaching.

Certification courses are meant to expand the knowledge and skills of students. Once your students finish their course, they can add this certification to their resume to make them more attractive to employers. These days, there are many options for free certification courses. Of course, if you will teach such a course, you will still be paid by the company that employs you. Whether your students pay for the course or not, you still have to provide your students with everything they need to ensure that they are prepared for future employment.

Since most students who take certification courses are interested in finding employment afterward, these courses are typically skills-focused and career-oriented. This means that aside from teaching your students the skills they need to succeed, you may also include a few lessons about how they can find a great job where they can practice everything they have learned. As an online teacher for such a course, you must know exactly what skills your students need to learn and what additional concepts, lessons or information you need to teach them.

It would also be a good idea for you to ask your students what their plans are after they graduate from the course you are teaching. For instance, if your students plan to use your course to help them get a degree in the future, you might advise them to check that the course you are teaching is transferable and that the credit will be honored at the school they plan to attend. This is valuable advice that most students might not even think about as they would only focus on the course itself.

Often, online and offline certification courses are associated with certain labor-intensive skills like welding, plumbing, and automotive repairs. However, these courses aren't limited to such careers. Since this type of online course is becoming more popular, schools have started offering certifications in various professional arenas like computer technology, healthcare, and even education. Although getting a degree is still one of the best options for students, taking a certification course is very popular, especially because students can complete it in a shorter amount of time.

In the past, most certification courses were done in a classroom. But thanks to the technological advancements in recent years, students can now complete these certifications online. As an online teacher, this is advantageous for you, especially if you have the skills, knowledge, and ability to teach specific certification courses.

ONLINE DEGREE COURSES

Degree online courses are now becoming popular for students all over the world as a way to earn their undergraduate degrees. Online degree courses are perfect for students who won't have the time to attend full-time classes on-campus. This option is also suitable for students who have already obtained their undergraduate degree online and they want to further their education. This is another type of online course that is flexible as it focuses more on self-paced learning.

As a teacher of an online degree course, you have two options. First, you can teach the same subjects for students who are studying different courses. Second, you can teach different subjects for students who are studying the same course. The first option is easier as you won't have to prepare different activities or lessons. The second option, however, allows you to get to know your students better as you will be teaching different subjects to them.

If you are employed by a university, the management might assign you a workload based on your skills, knowledge, and abilities. In such a case, things might be much easier for you as you would just have to follow the curriculum or syllabus given to you by your school. All you have to do is to think about how you will present the lessons unless this information is also provided to you. Because of the flexibility of degree courses, this option is probably the most versatile one. As long as the university has received accreditation to offer degree courses, practically any degree can be earned by students online.

SHORT AND NANO ONLINE COURSES

Short online courses are simple, short, and they offer a way for students to learn various topics that they are interested in. Typically, these courses last for a couple of weeks or a few months which means that students don't have to invest too much time and effort in them. When students enroll in short courses, they would only have to attend online classes for a few hours each week. This means that as a teacher of an online short course, you can teach several students a day.

These days, people of all ages who have some free time in their schedules may opt to sign up for an online short course. The convenience of being able to learn something new without having to physically go to a school is the biggest appeal of such courses. As students take various short courses, they can potentially find the career path that they will follow for the foreseeable future. As a teacher, knowing that you have contributed to this is an amazing feeling.

Although short online courses are very convenient, easy, and educational, students don't always get certificates at the end. As with the MOOCs, you can ask the school or company you're working for if such a certificate will be given to your students at the end of the course. This is an advantage for students as they can include the certificate on their resume when applying for jobs.

While short online courses are... short, nano online courses are even shorter. By nature, these courses are very easy for students to learn. Also, the topics of these courses are a lot simpler. For instance, when they sign up for nano courses, students can learn life skills, simple educational topics or even tips and tricks to help them overcome real-world problems. Typically, nano courses only last for a couple of hours up to two weeks. Because of their simplicity and short durations, these also happen to be the cheapest types of online courses students can take.

Students in high school or college can take nano courses as a way to review before taking significant exams. They can also opt for these courses right before they take entrance exams to universities or even board exams. As a teacher of a nano course, you should already have a plan for how you will teach everything your students have to know within a very short period of time. That way, you can be sure that your students will always get the most out of the nano courses that you teach them.

For both short online courses and nano online courses, the biggest advantages are convenience and flexibility. Students can simply go online and learn what they need to at their most convenient time. If you want to teach short and nano courses, you would have to arrange your schedule well so that your classes don't overlap with one another. These courses also provide your students with a unique experience, whether they are done individually or in small groups. As long as you can come up with engaging and interesting ways to present the topics, students will keep coming to learn from you.

SYNCHRONOUS ONLINE COURSES

Synchronous online courses are the exact opposite of asynchronous online courses as you would be conducting your classes at the same time even if your students are from different locations. While conducting simultaneous, real-time online classes, you will interact with your students, they will interact with you, and you can also give them opportunities to interact with each other. While conducting this type of course, you can make the most out of web conferencing apps and other online tools to make your classes more interesting. Having tried out a few, I recommend one that has handy teachers for teachers like muting your whole class and raising hands.

When students enroll in a synchronous online course, they have to follow a certain schedule. If it's time for you to teach the class, your students have to show up virtually. These classes are a lot like webinars where you and your students can interact with each other through video and audio or through a chat room that is typically built into most web conferencing tools. This type of online course is highly interactive, engaging, and it allows students to learn in real time.

The great thing about synchronous online courses is that you can plan fun activities for your students even if you are teaching in a virtual classroom. You will also be able to deal with your students' issues as they arise. For instance, if you are introducing a new concept that most of your students cannot understand, right there and then, you can take note of their reactions or feedback, and at the end of your class, you can come up with a new way to introduce the lesson or reinforce it. If such a situation occurs in an asynchronous online class, it would take more time for you to realize that the lesson you have taught wasn't understood by your students. Only then will you be able to come up with a new plan to help your students out.

Of course, this method comes with its own set of downsides, especially for students. For one, students have to stick with the schedule that you (or your school) has set for them. This means that if some of your students come from places that have different time zones, they have to adjust to the schedule. Of course, if all of your students come from the same country or state as you, this won't be an issue. Late arrivals also disrupt the class.

Another main issue with this type of online course is when you encounter technical difficulties with your device. For instance, you are in the middle of your class, and your computer freezes.

If you don't have a backup device, you have to fix the issue before you can go back to your class. However, if you can't fix the issue right away, you would have wasted a lot of time with troubleshooting. This can be very frustrating, especially if you were in the middle of a very engaging discussion with your students. The same thing goes for your students. If their devices crash or if they experience technical difficulties in the middle of your class, they might not be able to finish it. For such issues, it's best to have a backup plan. You can even tell your students to come up with their own backup plan for such issues so that they don't end up missing valuable class time.

TRANSFORMATION ONLINE COURSES

Transformation online courses involve gaining a deeper knowledge of a certain topic or course. As an online teacher, you will help your students understand a topic, method, process or course in a more profound way. In this type of online course, you will focus on the results, not the process.

When teaching a transformation course online, you will guide your students through the course and help them learn everything that they need to find success in the future. As a teacher, one of the best advantages of these courses is that they can be quite complex, so you can be paid very well for them. But due to the nature of these courses, it would take a lot of time and effort on your part to create the plans for these courses. Even while teaching, you also have to prepare more as you have to provide enough learning materials on the hosting platform of your online course.

For instance, you have to record high-quality videos in terms of content and resolution—then upload these for your students to access. You must keep uploading content, especially if your topic or course tends to change over time. For example, if you are teaching a transformation course in Cyber Security. The strategies you teach today would be very different from the strategies you would teach in six months because cyber security risks will change by then. This means that as a teacher of a transformative course, you should also make an effort to learn constantly so that you can refine your strategies and the content of your courses.

For transformative online courses, students can either enroll in registered courses or self-directed courses. For the first option, your students would have to go online and attend your online classes aside from going through the learning materials that you provide. For the self-directed option, this is similar to the individual learning courses where students would simply access the learning materials you provide. Then they would learn the concepts at their own pace. Either way, your students would have to finish the course in a specific amount of time that may range from a couple of hours to a few weeks or months. Although these courses are quite intense, they seldom last long.

WEB-BASED AND WEB-ENHANCED ONLINE COURSES

Web-based online courses are exclusively delivered online from start to finish. This means that they are excellent options for students who want to get their degree from a different country. Most distance and remote learning is done through web-based online courses. Here, you will use all of the online tools and resources provided by your school to introduce lessons, conduct classes, and give assessments. You will also have to learn how to use the many online platforms for web-based courses available out there. This type of online course involves both online classes and giving access to your students to learn lessons online.

On the other hand, a web-enhanced online course involves meeting your students at a set schedule for you to talk about the most important points of the module you provide. You would set the date and time for this meeting. After the online meeting where you discuss the module and other learning materials, your students can access the resources you provide whenever they want. This means that web-enhanced online courses are also student-based as the students can learn at their own pace. Whether you plan to teach a web-based online course or a web-enhanced online course, here are some steps to help you start off:

- First, set the learning goals of your course. These will

guide you as you think of the lessons to teach, the learning materials you create, and the activities you will give to your students.

- Know your audience. If you will be teaching a certain course, you will be exposed to certain types of students who have similar expectations. For instance, if you will teach a web-based online course for web design, then you will be teaching students who are interested in learning the basics of creating websites. These students would be looking for unique tips, strategies, and knowledge that will help them land a job in the future. Once you understand this, it becomes easier for you to create plans that will engage your students while moving them towards the learning goals.

- Choose the platforms, software, and online tools to use for your course. These days, there are so many options to choose from. Later, we will be discussing these in detail. If something catches your interest, you can research more about it to determine if you can use it for your course. The software and online tools you choose also need to be user-friendly for your audience. If this is younger children, you need to consider the parents who may have to use the technology too.

- Start creating plans and content for your students. Since web-based and web-enhanced online classes involve students accessing learning materials on their own, you must provide what they need. Make sure that all of the content you create is relevant, interesting, and will help your students learn what they need to by the end of the course.

- Keep track of your students' progress. This will help you determine if your online interactions and the learning materials you provide are effective. It will also allow you to identify students who might need more help and reinforcement to catch up with the course. Keeping track of your students' progress also makes assessments much easier for you when it's almost time for your students to graduate from your course. Just because we are moving everything online doesn't mean that you need a fancy digital system. I still keep a notepad next to me to make notes during classes because I only want my computer to be used for the class. At the end of my day, I upload all my notes.

4

THE BEST METHODS AND PRACTICES FOR ONLINE TEACHING

At this point, you should already have a deeper understanding of online teaching. Now, it's time to start learning the practical aspects of this teaching method. As you start teaching in digital classrooms and virtual settings, you will discover new and exciting things that you have never experienced in traditional classrooms. For you to become an effective online teacher, you must learn how to "go with the flow" by employing the right strategies. This chapter is all about these strategies.

Whether you will be employed by a school or a company that offers educational courses, you will gain access to all of the resources they have. Of course, there are countless resources online too. Combine all of these together and you can handle any course load no matter how comprehensive it is. Before moving on to the more detailed tips and strategies, let's go through some general advice to keep in mind:

- Don't focus too much on the "virtual classroom" as it might make you feel intimidated. Instead, focus more on the methods you will use and the activities you will do to make your lessons fun and engaging. It's going to be nerve wrecking at first but take the nerves away by enjoying yourself— just like the first day in a classroom.

- Learn as much as you can about online teaching tools so that you can determine which ones will help you out the most. Usually, you have to use different tools when teaching different courses or subjects. So, if you are assigned something new, find as many tools as you can then pick the best ones to use.

- Make sure that everything you use in your online teaching is high quality. From your device (laptop, computer or tablet) to your audio equipment, and internet connection, everything should work well so that you don't have to deal with distractions or technical issues.

- Learn how to manage your time. This is especially important if you teach courses where you only meet your students online once in a while. Make the most out of the time you spend teaching your students online. That way, they will find it easier to learn and understand the educational materials you provide. Whenever possible, schedule them for when your family are at work/school.

- Make sure that all of the learning materials you provide are accessible to all of your students. If needed, you can send sample materials first then ask your students to confirm if they have received those materials. If students appear and they don't have the materials, use the chat to share them during the class. It's faster than trying to send it again. You can even ask your students to send you a simple confirmation each time you post or upload something new so that you're sure that all of your students get what they need.

Finally, you should also learn how to motivate your students to learn even if you only interact in a virtual classroom. This is very important, especially if you teach courses that encourage self-paced learning. If you can keep your students motivated, you won't have to worry about them learning independently. By the end of your course, they would have already learned what they need. As you go through this chapter, you will learn more strategies that will help you improve student engagement, deliver your classes in better ways, and become a more effective online teacher overall.

ONLINE TEACHING MADE EASY

As an online teacher, you should always be on the lookout for ways to improve your methods and engage your students. Remember that your main goal is to guide your students, provide what they need, and help them overcome challenges on their way to attaining their learning goals. Since online teaching doesn't always involve real-time interaction, you may have to put in more effort to ensure that your students are making progress as time goes by.

Before you can start refining your methods, you must first establish a basic structure for teaching students online. From the moment you start your first online class, you should already have a plan of action. Just like teaching a traditional classroom, you can ensure the best possible outcomes if you think about what to do before you face your students. In this chapter, you will learn all of the basic—and most effective—strategies to make online teaching easy even if you are a beginner. Create a structure and a smooth flow for your online class by doing the following:

Establish Your Presence and Authority

Just as online teaching may be new for you, it might also be a new thing for most of your students, especially if they have always enrolled in traditional schools. When students attend online classes, they might not know what to expect. They might have some ideas in their minds but if you want to make things clear for them, you must establish your presence and authority.

Establishing your presence means that you should help your students understand that you will always be there for them— since you are the teacher. Aside from the online classes, inform your students that you are available to guide them, answer questions, and give them advice as needed. Do this by sending emails, creating chat rooms, posting announcements, and opening special online forums for your students. You can also establish your presence by making sure to provide a wide range of learning materials throughout the course.

On the other hand, I would advise you to set clear working hours. Many other teachers and I have run into problems with students and or parents sending emails and messages at all times of the day, which is fine until they expect a reply. For your own sake, you need to establish your working hours and a work-life balance.

As for your authority, you can do this by making it clear that you are the teacher. Instead of telling your students that they must respect you because of your position, show them why they should respect you. From the first day, you must put your best foot forward so that your students will feel impressed and motivated. Also, make sure to show your professionalism at all times. As long as your students understand that you are the teacher and they should listen to you, online teaching will become easier.

Welcome Your Students and Orient Them

During your very first online class, you should welcome your students with warmth and enthusiasm. If your students see that you're an approachable teacher who appreciates open communication, there is a higher likelihood that they will interact and communicate with you better. After welcoming them, it's time to orient your students about the class. Explain how online learning differs from traditional learning and this means that they will have to do things a bit differently. Here are some things you may want to include in your orientation on the first day:

- Establish a routine, especially if you have a course that involves regular online classes.
- Provide your students with a detailed syllabus that they will use as a guide throughout the course. You may also introduce the learning objectives of your course to help your students understand what is expected of them in terms of academics.
- Talk about your expectations in terms of online etiquette, communication, and participation in class.
- Emphasize the importance of due dates, especially when it comes to submitting their work.
- Explain to your students how you plan to provide them with learning materials. For instance, will you send these materials through email or will you upload them on Google Drive? Either way, you need to know

all of your students' email addresses. For the former, you will send the materials directly. For the latter, you will send the Google Drive link to all of your students and make sure that you grant access to them.

- Provide your students with basic troubleshooting tips. For this, you have to learn everything about the online tools you use so that you can teach your students how to deal with technical difficulties.

You can present anything else that you think is necessary for your students to understand before you start the learning process. While orienting your students, encourage them to ask questions, especially if something isn't clear to them. Also, try to present your orientation in a fun and engaging way. That way, your students will look forward to their next classes with you.

Encourage a Supportive Community and Nurture This

One of the biggest challenges of online learning is the risk that your students will feel isolated as they are trying to learn new things. Although some students thrive by learning on their own, most students need constant guidance. This is why you should encourage a supportive community. You can do this by openly communicating with your students that you are there to support them in whatever way they need. Think about setting aside some time just to talk and get to know each other. Plan icebreaking activities for the first session so that people begin to feel more relaxed and comfortable.

You can also encourage your students to help each other out, especially when you aren't available to provide support (although this shouldn't happen often). If you notice that your students have established this type of community, make sure to nurture it by encouraging your students to help each other out or ask for help from you when they need to.

Build Relationships With Each of Your Students

In line with the previous tip, you can create a supportive community by establishing relationships with each of your students. The best way to do this is by setting one-on-one schedules where you can communicate and interact with your students individually and without distractions. Some ways to do this are by starting a discussion board, sending them emails, and personalizing your responses to them whenever possible. The key here is to communicate with your students so that they don't see you as a threat but as a person who is always there to support them. If you have suddenly switched to online teaching, don't forget the activities that you did in class to build relationships, maybe things like celebrating birthdays.

Explain That Your Students Will Have to Do a Lot of Work to Succeed

By now, you already understand that online teaching is different from teaching in a classroom. Now, it's time for you to help your students understand this. If your students were used to just sitting in a classroom whole only half-listening to their teacher, they have to change their ways. After all, your interactions won't occur as frequently. So, you should make most of your online sessions by encouraging all of your students to participate actively.

This is very important, especially if half or more than half of their course involves independent learning. Your students have to work extra hard to understand the lessons, accomplish their projects, and reach their learning goals.

Think Before You Post, Upload or Share

While it's important for you to post, upload or share content regularly, you must think about what you create very carefully first before you make anything accessible to your students. Remember that you are the teacher in this setup. This means that sending out something that is riddled with errors might make your students wonder why they should continue listening to you. On the other hand, if you always send content that is engaging, well-made, and error-free, your students will always feel inspired to keep learning.

Provide Resources That Are Readily Accessible to Everyone

After perfecting the content, it's time to share what you have made. As part of your online teaching plans, decide how you will be sharing the learning content you create. Since you will be teaching an online course, the best way to do this is online. You can use different platforms and methods depending on the material you will share. For instance, if you want to share digital publications for your students to study, you can simply share the link. If you plan to share PowerPoint presentations, upload these on Google Drive and give your students access to the drive. Just make sure that the materials are readily accessible to all of your students to ensure that nobody gets left behind.

Have a Good Balance of Individual and Group Activities

As part of your plans, try to incorporate individual and group activities. While individual learning is already a given, thinking of group activities might be a bit more challenging. But these types of activities are more interesting for students. You can have online debates, group discussions, chat sessions in chat rooms, online forums, and discussion boards. Find the right balance between these two types of learning to keep your students motivated.

Always Close Your Online Classes Well

Even though you will conduct your classes online, you should still find memorable ways to close or end them. Simple summaries are okay once in a while but you can also try assigning activities or asking reflective questions before ending your classes. This is another amazing way to engage your students, especially if you make this part of your routine.

Regularly Ask for Feedback From Your Students

Finally, it's very helpful for you to ask for regular feedback from your students. By doing this, you can keep modifying, revising, and improving your methods, activities, and even your teaching style to suit your students' needs. You can create a discussion board for this or use any other method that you see fit. Encourage your students to be as honest as possible. And if any of them give you constructive criticism, accept it with grace.

LEVELING UP YOUR ONLINE TEACHING SKILLS

By following the tips above, you can come up with a smooth structure for your online classes. Having such a structure will make it easier for you to focus on your lessons and your students. As time goes by, you will be experiencing the reality of online classes. With every class you teach, you will learn new things, gain new experiences, and discover what strategies work best—and what strategies don't work as well. You should try taking some time at the end of each class (or each day) to reflect on everything you have learned, especially if this is your first time teaching online.

Learning through experience is very effective. But it will also be very beneficial for you if you already have knowledge of specific methods and techniques to use. As I researched online learning and experienced it firsthand, I discovered that some methods are more effective than others. Let us go through these methods to give you an idea of how you can plan your lessons and approach online teaching.

Demonstration

Before becoming a teacher, you would have already experienced giving a teaching demo. Typically, those who apply for a teaching job would have to present a lesson in front of the school's hiring team. That way, they can determine if you are the right fit for the school. During a teaching demo, you will show them what you are capable of, not just by talking but by showing or "demonstrating" too.

When it comes to teaching, demonstrations are similar to this. They involve showing your students something while you are explaining. For instance, if you want to show your students how to make an art project, you will be showing them each step as you tell them about it. Demonstrating is a very effective method of teaching, especially when teaching younger children. For instance, if you are a preschool teacher and you are tasked to teach online, you may have to do several demonstrations a week. This is because a lot of children cannot follow directions merely after hearing them. You would have to show them what to do as well. This encourages young children to work independently.

Before conducting demonstrations in class, you must know what you need to do first. You must know the lesson, the age group of the students, the resources that will be available to you, and the resources or materials that you need to prepare. For demonstrations, preparation is one of the most important parts. Here are some steps to guide you when preparing for a demonstration:

Familiarize yourself with the topic or activity

For instance, you want your students to make their own booklet wherein they draw the life cycle of a butterfly. Before you can teach this, you should learn the stages of the life cycle, the correct terms used (like larva, cocoon, and chrysalis, among others), and even how to make simple illustrations for each of the stages.

Make a list of the materials you need and prepare them

Now that you have an activity in mind, it's time to think of what your students will need to complete it. In a traditional classroom, you have to prepare everything for your students, especially for activities such as the one used in the example above. Since you will be teaching online, you may ask your students to prepare some of the materials for it.

Going back to the example, if you want your students to make a booklet with their own illustrations of the stages, ask them to prepare materials like paper, scissors, pencils, glue, coloring materials, and a stapler or fastener to bind the pages of the booklet together. You won't be able to help your students if the list you give them isn't complete. This is why it's important for you to write down all of the materials you need for the demo.

Practice the activity first

When preparing your materials for the activity, it's a good idea to prepare two sets for yourself. I confess, I sat in front of a mirror a couple of times! One set will be used for your practice run and the second set will be used for the actual lesson. With the materials you need, practice demonstrating the lesson. If you want to see how well you demonstrate, record yourself while you practice. Then watch your recording to see if you missed anything or if you demonstrated the activity flawlessly.

If you have become more experienced as an online teacher, you may skip this step. But for your first few demonstrations, it's better to practice to calm your nerves and make you feel more confident.

Demonstrate the activity to your students

Finally, demonstrate the activity in your virtual classes. Although unexpected things may happen such as some students might not prepare all of the materials they need or your students might take too long with one of the steps, the important thing is that you are prepared. After the demonstration, you can supplement your activity with interesting things like a video of a butterfly coming out of a cocoon, pictures of different butterflies or even a real butterfly that you caught from the garden.

Demonstrations are very interesting for students, especially if you can conduct them well. This is also a very personal method of teaching as you would be speaking directly to your students to ensure that you are guiding them in the best way possible.

Discussion

Basic as this method is, it remains to be highly effective both in traditional classes and online classes. But the difference is that discussions in an online class can be done either through a virtual class using the "traditional method" or through discussion boards. The traditional method involves discussing and interacting with your students during your online class. This method is simple, effective, and it works.

The second method is a bit more complicated and it involves a discussion board. This is a general term used for virtual "bulletin boards" where you and your students can communicate with each other by leaving messages online. Through these discussion boards, you can share topics, lessons, and even links to learning materials. Discussion boards are very interesting for students and they offer flexibility for both of you. When using discussion boards to facilitate discussions, here are some tips to guide you:

Set the rules and expectations

Although discussion boards are interesting and fun, they can also be an avenue for students to start disrespecting each other or even you. To avoid this, you should set the rules and expectations for your discussion boards. Make sure that your students understand that students should follow basic 'netiquette'.

They should always show respect in terms of the messages they are sending. Make it clear that bullying isn't allowed. Also, make it clear that the discussion board is only meant for sending messages about the course or topic you're discussing. This means that your students shouldn't send personal messages on the discussion boards that aren't related to your topics. As long as you set these rules, it becomes easier for you to manage your discussion boards and keep them professional.

Provide your students with a structure for your discussions

Aside from the basic rules, you should also provide your students with a structure for your discussion boards. Through this structure, your students will get a better understanding of what discussion boards are and how to use them. The structure you provide can come in the form of a syllabus or an outline of the topics that you will discuss throughout your course.

Think about how many students you can handle

One of the best features of a discussion board is being able to teach a large group of students at a time, this might also depend on the age of the students. However, you must also determine whether you can manage a large class or one with fewer students. To get the most out of your discussions, you should be able to communicate and interact with all of the students individually. If your class is too big, you might not be able to do this. For the first few online discussions or discussion boards you do, you may want to start with a few students. Once you get the hang of things, you may start accepting more.

Encourage your students to take notes

Whether you are conducting online discussions or you are communicating with your students through a discussion board, it would be very helpful to encourage them to take notes. Note taking is an important part of learning as the action helps students retain information better. By taking down notes, they can pick out the most important parts of your discussions and use these for when it's time for them to take assessments.

Offer alternatives to discussion boards too

Although discussion boards are highly interactive and effective, there are other methods you can use to conduct class discussions online. Instead of being the only one introducing topics or teaching concepts, create discussion groups where your students will talk about a certain topic and take turns discussing.

Students must learn how to work as a team even if they attend online classes. Help your students understand the dynamics of a team so that they find it easier to work together. Ask them to choose leaders for their team discussions and make sure that everyone gets an opportunity to speak up.

Make sure that the discussions go both ways

One-way discussions tend to be very boring, especially if nothing else happens. To make sure that your students are always interested and engaged in your discussions, mix things up, and always encourage your students to keep up their end of the discussion. You can do this by asking questions, letting them take turns, asking students to summarize the learning and, of course, through group discussions.

Provide coaching and feedback

Apart from leading and facilitating discussions, it's also your responsibility to coach your students and provide feedback regularly. Teach them how to use the discussion boards, how to hold the attention of the other students when it's their turn to discuss, and even how to use the online tools they need for their classes.

By coaching them, you are also helping your students become independent learners, which ultimately, makes it easier for you to facilitate your online classes. Also, you should give feedback to your students whenever you feel it is necessary. For instance, if you think that one of your students isn't participating enough, then you can approach them privately to give them feedback about their performance and ask them if they need any help.

Assess your students' learning

It's very important to keep track of your students' progress. Come up with a grading system, give them regular assessments, and observe them whenever they are conducting discussions. Assessments are an important aspect of learning, whether online or in traditional classrooms.

Finally, when it comes to class discussions, you should also know when it's time for you to stop posting online. Once you are done with your topic, you shouldn't be posting on the discussion board anymore. It's time for you to sit back and read the messages that your students post. Then when it's time for a new topic, that's when you should start posting again.

Gamification

In Chapter 1, you have already been introduced to the term "'gamification," a method of teaching where you use games and fun activities to introduce your lessons. Personally, I have used this method so many times and it has always been well received. Sites like Wisc Online allow you to create your own games. I have a number of games that I have created that I know I can use for different classes. Of course, when you tell your students that you will be playing a game, they will surely feel excited. Before we go through some tips and gamification strategies, here are the benefits of this method:

- It encourages your students to be more involved in the process of learning.
- It encourages your students to think outside of the box.
- It encourages teamwork, collaboration, and a friendly sense of competition.
- It helps your students develop new skills apart from the concepts that you teach.

Basically, gamification makes your teaching methods more fun. And when fun is involved, students learn more effectively. Now, let's go through some tips, strategies, and ideas for you to incorporate this method into your online teaching:

Allow your students to choose the activities

No matter what age your students are, they would have probably been exposed to different types of online games. If you have prepared different types of games for your students, you can give them the opportunity to choose which games to play. This is a powerful motivator for students.

Create quests or challenges for your students

When it comes to online games, there is nothing more fun than a quest or a challenge. These types of games take longer and they give your students opportunities to invest in your lessons as they become more engaged with the quests or challenges. This is also an excellent way to conduct progressive or independent learning.

Offer rewards like badges and bonus points

To stay with the theme of gamification, you can come up with a grading system that incorporates badges, bonus points, and other game-related gimmicks. Although you can follow the "traditional" grading system, assigning such terms to their grades will make things even more fun and interesting for your students.

Provide feedback instantly

When you play online games, you immediately know whether you succeed, fail or can progress on to the next level. Therefore, if you plan to use gamification, you may want to provide feedback to your students in the same way. For instance, after accomplishing an activity, you can allow your students to either move forward with more challenging lessons or remain in the same "level" where you give them different activities to reinforce what they have already learned. Do this if you don't think that your students have mastered the skill or concept.

There are so many different types of games that you can introduce to your students as an online teacher. Even if you use other methods, you can still incorporate fun games and activities to increase engagement. Some examples of games that work well with online classes are:

- Puzzles like word puzzles, logic, charades or riddles.
- Question games like game shows, trivia games or word treasure hunts.
- Quizzes like those which your students will do against each other or in groups.
- Role-playing where you will ask your students to come up with situations and dialogues to explain certain concepts or topics.
- Table-top games like Scrabble, dominoes, or Monopoly.
- Team games that encourage collaboration and friendly competition.
- ... and so much more.

As long as you can find online games to connect to the concepts you want to teach, you can use these to make things more fun for your students and for yourself too.

Hands-On Courses

By nature, online learning isn't as hands-on as learning in a traditional classroom. However, hands-on learning can still be possible, especially for science-oriented subjects where students learn better when they experience things for themselves. For instance, if you want to introduce a concept to students by explaining it to them, some might listen but there is a very big chance that a lot of your students might find other things to do while "listening" to you. By the end of your lesson, only the few students who truly listened would have understood the concept you taught.

On the other hand, if you introduced the same concept by first conducting an experiment with your students, this will grab their attention right away. The good news is that you can still do this even as an online teacher. First of all, you must have all of the materials and equipment you need to conduct such activities. In most cases, you would have to conduct your online classes in school even if your students are at home. That way, you don't have to purchase the equipment and materials you need to intrigue your students through hands-on activities. Apart from this, here are a few more tips for you to incorporate hands-on courses:

Consider using virtual labs

These days, there are online resources for virtually anything— even virtual labs. With such tools, your students can experience simulations, virtual experiments, and even video demonstrations of interesting scientific procedures and activities. If you don't think that you can conduct the experiments for your students or that it's too complicated for students to prepare the materials and equipment at home, take advantage of these tools to make the experience more hands-on for your students even if it's just in a virtual way.

Research simple experiments that your students can do at home

If you can find ways for students to conduct experiments at home, this will be a wonderful hands-on experience for them. Just make sure that the experiments you assign to your students are simple, interesting, and safe. Also, if your students are minors, make sure to inform the parents of your plans so that they can facilitate the experiments. Prior to the date of the experiment, send your students a list of materials they need. Also, send a list of rules for conducting experiments. This activity requires both hands-on and demonstration methods to pull it off successfully.

Find other ways to encourage interaction

Apart from experiments and virtual tools, you can also find other ways to encourage your students to interact with you, with the other students, and with the lessons. For instance, you can tell a story where your students will participate by playing the different characters. Or you can incorporate movements and physical activities into your lessons. Find activities where your students experience things using their senses instead of simply sitting in front of a computer while listening to you.

Hands-on courses and learning methods are very interesting. But they do involve a lot of planning too. But if you use these methods frequently, they become easier for you and soon, you will become a more effective and interesting teacher.

Lecture-Based Courses

Lecture-based courses and teaching methods are still very effective even though many people see these as 'boring'. But when you need to teach subjects like history, conducting lectures is the best way to go. When it comes to lectures, you can either conduct them live or you can also record your lectures and upload your videos online. Again, the key here is to find ways to make your lectures more interesting so that your students will feel motivated to listen. Here are some tips for you:

Conduct live lectures

Before conducting a live lecture, make sure to study the concept you will teach very well. There is nothing worse than being called out by one of your students because you shared inaccurate or incomplete information. Being asked questions that you don't know the answers to can also make you feel very stressed.

If you want your lectures to go smoothly, you need to feel confident. Preparation can help you with this. Also, you may want to practice your lectures a couple of times to know how much time you need. Try practicing in front of your laptop with your webcam on so that you can position yourself correctly and determine how engaging you are as a speaker.

Pre-record your lectures and upload them

Although pre-recording your lectures won't require as much confidence, you should still prepare for these if you want to save a lot of time and effort. Imagine how frustrating it would be if you had to keep stopping your recording because you missed some concepts or you hadn't prepared all of the materials you needed. Then instead of being able to upload your pre-recorded lecture right away, you still have to edit it to make sure that it flows smoothly.

One thing to remember in terms of pre-recorded lectures is that they don't involve interactions. This means that you have to be doubly sure that you have conducted your lectures in an interesting and engaging way. Watch your pre-recorded video first before uploading it to make sure that it's complete, interesting, and it's neither too long nor too short.

Learn how to engage your students

Whether you plan to conduct live or pre-recorded lectures, the key is to engage your students. That way, you will catch—and maintain—their attention no matter how seemingly boring your topic is. Research about your topic, prepare your lecture and fine-tune it.

Of course, engaging your students is much easier when conducting live lectures. For these types of lectures, you can interact with your students, ask them questions, encourage them to ask questions (just make sure that you're ready to answer them), encourage your students to reflect while listening, and read the room. For instance, if you are fifteen minutes into your lecture and none of your students have reacted or interacted with you, then it might be time to ask a question. Don't fall into the trap of simply talking nonstop until the end of your session as this will surely make your students fall asleep!

Another effective thing you can do to improve your lecture courses or methods is to ask for feedback from your students. Ask them what they thought about your lectures, if they have suggestions for how you can improve, and even for topics that they want you to talk about that are related to your main lessons. Asking younger students is like opening Pandora's Box and you are likely to get some comical answers (I think we should play more games), but there could ideas that you can take away.

Simulation

Simulations involve allowing students to use a certain model of behavior for them to gain a better and deeper understanding of it. For instance, if you're teaching an economics class where your topic is e-commerce, an example of a simulation is to ask your students to "create" their own online shop and sell their products to the other students in the class. In such an activity, your students will experience being buyers, sellers, and even marketers. After the activity, you can talk about their experiences and what they learned through the simulation.

Using simulations is another amazing way for you to make things more interesting in your online class. Since simulations can also be done online, this method is easy to incorporate into online teaching. Instructional and experiential simulations can potentially engage your students in ways that ensure profound learning. This kind of learning empowers students and motivates them to keep moving forward until they have mastered a specific concept or skill. When it comes to simulations, there are three main elements you need to make them as effective as possible:

Preparation

Naturally, you have to prepare for the simulations or activities that you will do with your students. Before making a plan, decide whether you will conduct a role-playing simulation or a system-dynamic simulation. The first one involves your students taking on real-life roles for them to learn the concepts. The example shared above about creating an online shop falls into this category.

A system-dynamic simulation involves the use of computers. Instead of asking your students to experience the situations in real life, you would introduce them to an online tool that changes based on the decisions your students make on the tool. For instance, you can introduce them to simulation apps or games where they would have to reach a certain goal at the end. However, these types of simulations have a narrower scope since the outcomes are already coded into the program.

Whichever simulation method you choose, prepare everything you need for it. Learn about the simulation activity, plan it, create instructions for it, and orient your students on it before allowing them to start experiencing the simulations. This is especially important if your students have never experienced simulations before. Otherwise, you will spend a lot of time asking questions and explaining things over and over again because your students don't know what they are expected to do!

Participation

After preparing everything you need for your simulation, it's time to bring your students into the simulated environment. Simulations work best when students are actively engaged in them. As your students participate, they should learn how to predict outcomes based on the decisions they make. Try to think of simulations that encourage students to become active learners instead of passive ones. Do this by planning interesting simulations that your students can connect to real-life situations.

Post-Simulation Reflection

After the simulation activity, it's time to have a discussion with your students. Before this, you should already have a list of questions to ask your students. The post-simulation discussion is your opportunity to deepen your students' learning through discussions and reflections. If you can find ways to connect what they have learned to real life, that would be even better.

5

ONLINE TEACHING TOOLS TO MAKE YOUR LIFE EASIER

We have already defined online teaching, differentiated it from classroom teaching, and we have also gone through a wealth of information about the most practical and effective teaching strategies you can use. Now, let us focus on the online teaching tools that will make your life easier.

As you will soon discover, this chapter is very straightforward. Here, you will learn about the most effective online tools that will enable you to conduct your classes. These tools will either help you prepare for your class or help you carry out your class depending on what kind of assistance you need. Also, remember that these tools are the best ones at the time of this book's writing. In a few months or years, new tools may emerge so it's important for you to always be on the lookout for such things.

BASIC DIGITAL CLASSROOM TOOLS

When finding online tools that will help make your life easier, you should start with the most basic ones. These tools will help you transition from classroom teaching to blended teaching, and finally, to online teaching. Here are some of the best options available. You can even use some of these for other tasks apart from using them as basic online teaching tools.

Edmodo

Edmondo is an online tool that gets assimilated into a social network for the purpose of connecting you with your students. Here, you can provide learning materials, create groups for students to collaborate with each other, and even keep track of your students' performances.

HotChalk

HotChalk is an educational virtual environment where you can connect with your students, as well as their parents. Here, you can store and share your curriculum, syllabus, handouts, assessments, and other important school files. It's a free online tool with enough features to make it valuable.

Projeqt

Projeqt is an online tool where you can create online quizzes, videos, multimedia presentations, and other types of learning materials. You can share these with your students and the tool will adapt your materials visually to the devices that your students are using.

Pumpic

Pumpic is a highly versatile online tool for monitoring. It focuses on connecting you with your students through GPS or iCloud monitoring. This is very helpful, especially if you have younger students so that you can always provide updates to their parents. It has other unique features too that make it suitable for teaching different age groups.

Socrative

Socrative is an online tool that allows you to create educational games or exercises. Then you can share these with your students no matter what device they are using. This tool also allows you to make personalized learning materials for students who are either advanced or those who have to catch up with others.

Teachem

Teachem is an online web-based service where you can customize YouTube videos by adding flashcards, notes, and even quizzes to them. This interactive tool allows you to teach different subjects using videos as one of your main learning materials.

TED-Ed

TED-Ed is an online educational platform where you can collaborate with teachers, animators, and even students to create your lessons. You can also share your ideas for when other teachers, animators, and students need help.

Thinglink

Thinglink allows you to create images that your students interact with. Do this by adding photos, sounds, text, and music. After creating these learning materials, you can share them with your students through social media platforms.

DIGITAL CLASSROOM TOOLS FOR K-12

Managing a digital classroom doesn't have to be a challenge, especially if you use the right tools to help you out. This next set of tools will help you become a master at classroom management as an online teacher.

Blackboard

Blackboard is online software that is web based and highly educational. Here, you can create your own virtual classroom, manage the courses you teach, and even combine it with traditional methods for a blended learning experience.

Edpuzzle

Edpuzzle is the perfect option for when you like sharing a lot of videos with your students. In an online classroom, you have to make sure that students are engaged in the videos. With this online tool, they can interact with you while watching to make it easier to manage your students.

Google Classroom

Google Classroom is a free online tool that is highly accessible to everyone who needs it. Here, you can set up your own online class. It can be a live class where you interact with your students and share important information. If you need to upload learning materials, you can do so through Google Drive.

IXL

IXL allows you to set your standards for core subjects. This is an amazing option for when you are teaching an individual online course or any other online course that focuses on self-paced learning.

Moodle

Moodle provides you with an amazing learning platform that you and your students can access anywhere at any time. Here, you can manage a class made up of students from all over the world. It is so popular that it is even translated in over 120 different languages.

Nearpod

Nearpod is an amazing online tool for presenting different types of learning materials. Here, you can make your classes more interesting by adding games, questions, and other things that you think will add to the engagement of your students.

Quizizz

Quizizz is an online tool that helps make assessments easier while you teach online. Here, you can give quizzes, create flashcards, and even review previous concepts in a fun, game-based setting. This is another cool online tool to use along with gamification methods.

Zoom

Zoom is one of the most popular online web conferencing platforms now and for good reason. It is easy to use and it even offers breakout rooms where you can split your meeting into individual sessions. This means that you can conduct an online class while conducting individual conversations with students too.

TOOLS FOR UNIVERSITY AND COURSEWARE

As an online teacher for university students, online tools can help you out immensely. These tools play an important role in how you handle the class, how you present your lessons, and how effectively your students will learn. The great thing about these online tools is that you can use them for students of different ages too.

Animoto

Animoto is suitable for students of varying ages. You can use it and you can also teach your students how to use it. The main purpose of this tool is to create videos and photo slideshows for the purpose of learning.

Coursera

Coursera is suitable for older learners such as those in high school or college. This is a great tool for MOOCs as you can use it to stream lectures and even give your students opportunities to learn from educators from different schools.

Canvas

Canvas is a type of learning management platform that is also suitable for K-12 learning. This open-source online tool allows you to communicate with your students and provide them with the learning materials they need throughout your course.

Educreations

Educreations is an interactive screen casting and whiteboard tool that allows you to clearly explain different concepts within your virtual classrooms. Here, you can also reach out to your individual students to help them with their learning.

Haiku Deck

Haiku Deck is a digital tool that allows you to create presentations on your iPhone or iPad online. Here, you can utilize stock photos available on its huge database to create visual masterpieces for your lessons.

Loom

Loom is a simple online app that you can use to narrate, share, and even record lectures for your students. With this tool, you can even keep track of the students who have already watched your lectures so that you can remind those who haven't yet to do so.

Pear Deck

Pear Deck allows you to host slide presentations and even conduct assessments on the slides of your choice. While you are teaching, your students can enter notes, draw on your presentations, and do other things to help them understand your lessons better.

ONLINE LIBRARY RESOURCES

Although libraries these days are considered obsolete, you can keep up with the times by using online library resources. You can use these while planning your lessons and you can also suggest these resources to your students, especially if you have assigned them with research work or if they want to further their learning.

Booktrack

Booktrack is an excellent resource for students as it offers books for reading along with soundtracks to go with those books. This means that your students can learn better and retain information more effectively.

Learn Out Loud

Learn Out Loud is an amazingly huge content resource that you and your students can access freely. It offers courses, documentaries, and audiobooks for different ages and levels of learners. If you teach older students, this is an excellent option for individual learning courses.

INFOMINE

INFOMINE is a digital library that offers a wide range of resources. It offers articles, bulletin boards, eBooks, electric journals, and so much more. This makes it an amazing library resource for when you need to master a course before teaching it.

Internet Public Library

Internet Public Library is the very first digital public library made by and for the internet community. Here, you can access easy-to-find online resources as they are organized according to subject.

Intute

Intute is an online library resource where you can find information for subjects like humanities, arts, social sciences, technology, and science. It contains more than 100,000 records and it continues to grow.

SubjectsPlus

SubjectPlus is another amazing online resource that offers tons of subject guides. It has a simple interface and a responsive design that allows you to view it on browsers and on different devices too.

WhatShouldIReadNext.com

WhatShouldIReadNext.com is a valuable tool that you can use and suggest to your students. If you want to give reading assignments to reinforce the lessons you have introduced, this is an excellent option.

Whooo's Reading for Schools

Whooo's Reading for Schools is a highly motivational tool that allows you to involve your students in their learning progress. As they read the assignments you give, you can also keep track of your students' progress through this tool.

TOOLS FOR MANAGING VIDEO CONTENT

As an online teacher, making your own videos or sharing video content made by other educators should be part of your methods. Videos can be very interesting to students, especially when these are connected to the lessons they learn. Here are some of the best tools you can use for video content.

Brightcove

Brightcove offers a fantastic content management system (CMS) that you can use to manage the videos you create. With it, you can create video content and make modifications according to the needs of your students.

CMS Hub

CMS Hub enables you to upload videos to engage your students. With this online tool, you can easily manage your video content and even embed these into social media platforms, websites, and blog posts.

Genus Technologies

Genus Technologies is a unique online platform as you can use it to manage videos, images, documents, and even audio files. With this tool, you can share your video content to make it accessible to your students.

Haivision

Haivision is an online video platform that makes use of Secure Reliable Transport (SRT). It also offers an open-source technology for video streaming that allows you to create high quality videos to enhance your students' learning.

Kollective

Kollective is a cloud-based platform for content distribution that allows you to deliver content at a faster pace without requiring a lot of bandwidth. You can use this platform with different applications such as SCCM, Skype, and Stream.

MediaPlatform

MediaPlatform offers a unique integration of webcasts and video content that works seamlessly into Jive, SharePoint, and Yammer. You can even upload video content from other platforms then share these for your students to access them as needed.

Panopto

Panopto is one of the leading developers in the world of video content management. It's easy to use, highly flexible, and it allows you to create and share videos that will add to the impact of your lessons.

Zype

Zype is designed to make things easier for online teachers and students. Whether you need to create videos or distribute them, this online tool helps simplify the process. It even has clever features like metadata control, backups, and playlist structuring.

BLENDED LEARNING PLATFORMS

Remember that blended learning involves combining online teaching methods with traditional classroom methods. If you plan to transition into online teaching by first practicing blended learning, familiarize yourself with these tools. Then when you become an online teacher, you can continue using them.

Been for Education

Been for Education allows you to curate and browse the internet in a safe virtual environment. Here, you can collaborate with your students as you teach for the purpose of bringing your lessons to life.

G Suite for Education

G Suite for Education was formerly known as Google Apps for Education and this online tool will help improve your productivity as an online teacher. With this, you can manage your classwork while integrating online assessments, lessons, and topics for your students.

GoClass

GoClass helps you by improving your classroom management skills and enhancing your students' engagement. It offers various features that allow you to create content and make these accessible to your students.

Illuminate Education

Illuminate Education enables you to create content and share what you create for your students to see. Here, you can even create schedules, grading systems, and attendance records as part of your blended learning process.

Khan Academy

Khan Academy is one of the most popular online tools at the writing of this book. It offers countless practice exercises and instructional videos that you can use to make your classroom lessons and activities more interesting for your students.

LessonPaths

LessonPaths was formerly known as MentorMob and it allows you to create your own learning playlists. This works best for blended learning and flipped classrooms. Here, you can also allow your students to learn at their own pace.

Otus

Otus is one of the more recent additions to the online tool resources. You can use this free tool on your iPad to incorporate blended learning in your classroom. Here, you can give assessments, grade your students, record their attendance, and more.

PowerSchool

PowerSchool is another great tool that you can use to make your traditional classes a little more technological. You can use this to take attendance, track your students' progress, and even share data for your students or their parents to access.

READING TOOLS

Reading is one of the most important skills that students have to learn. As an online teacher, improving your reading skills allows you to become more effective in terms of researching, checking your students' work, and learning what you need to for your courses. These tools are some of the best ones you can use as an online teacher and as with the others, you can also suggest them to your students.

Diigo

Diigo allows you to annotate texts that you read online and save these for your reference. When you go back to the resources, you will see the tags, comments, and highlights in their links.

With this, you can create multiple libraries based on subjects or topics.

Feedly

Feedly automatically creates a list of all the articles that have been recently updated from the websites you follow. You can even use it for other resources that you follow like YouTube channels, podcasts, and Tumblr blogs, for example. With this, you can easily organize your reading content to make it easier for you to plan lessons.

GoodReader

This is a simple online resource that you can use for reading online sources, revise documents, highlight text, and perform other actions. You can also encourage your students to find interesting reads from this tool to nurture a love of reading in them.

iSpeech

iSpeech is a text to speech online tool that allows you to listen instead of read, making it perfect for when you have other things to do but you also need to catch up on your reading. Again, this is another great tool to suggest to your students as it even supports 20 different languages.

Pocket

Pocket is a simple app that you can use to manage your reading. It has a sleek design and is compatible with several platforms. With this, you can save interesting articles and texts to read at a later date—when you can focus better.

Readism

Readism is a cool app that allows you to determine your reading speed. This is an extension application in Chrome with a small timer at the bottom of your screen that indicates your reading time when you open an article. This tool is useful for you and your students, especially if you're trying to improve your reading speed.

Skitch

Skitch is a great online reading tool that allows you (or your students) to take photos of texts or images then highlight the important parts. As a teacher, you can use this to show your students which information or parts of the image to focus on. Your students can do the same to reinforce their learning.

Spritz

Spritz is an online speed reading app to help improve your reading speed through practice. With this, you can read a text without having to move your eyes. Instead, you will learn to read the words of a text one at a time. If you want to become a more efficient reader, this is the tool for you.

Oxford Owl

A particular favorite for younger students to teenagers as well as any students you may have whose first language isn't English. Students can choose from fiction and non-fiction books of all levels. Students can read along with playback. This is a great resource for phonetic work.

CLASSROOM MANAGEMENT TOOLS

As a classroom teacher, classroom management is an important thing. If you don't know how to manage your class, you won't be able to teach effectively. In the same way, you need to learn classroom management so that you can make the most of your online classes. Here are some of the best tools to help you out.

Bubbl

Bubbl is a mind-mapping tool that you can use for generating concepts and ideas for your classroom management. With this, you can make things more interesting for your students by creating activities, presentations, and discussions that will make it easier for you.

ClassDojo

ClassDojo is a simple and fun online tool that helps you manage the behaviors of your students to ensure that your classes are always on track. Using this tool, you can subtract points from your students when they behave negatively or give them bonus points for behaving in positive ways.

LanSchool Lite

LanSchool Lite is software for virtual classroom management that you can use to monitor your students better. It has a simple interface where you can see your students in real time.

MyVision Free

MyVision Free allows you to supervise your students in a virtual classroom. It also allows you to take control of your students' screen. This is very useful as you can opt to prevent them from using their screens if needed.

NetSupport School

NetSupport School is an award-winning software that enables you to interact with your students while monitoring them too. With this tool, you can also deliver your lessons, give assessments, and even collaborate with your students.

Stick Pick

Stick Pick enables you to manage your students better by differentiating your instruction. With this tool, you can categorize your students based on their learning levels. When you do this, the app matches your students to questions that are suited to their levels.

Veyon

Veyon is a virtual classroom management software that allows you to control the computers of your students so that you can present lessons, guide them while they work, and correct them as needed.

Wiggio

Wiggio is a collaborative tool that allows you to conduct virtual classes, create group messages for your students, share files, and more. While using this tool, you can keep track of your students' progress while they work to decrease distractions.

PARENT-TEACHER COMMUNICATION TOOLS

Communicating with parents is another essential aspect of online teaching, especially when teaching younger students. If you need to ask parents to prepare materials for complex activities, then you need to have a way to contact them. The same thing goes for when the parents of your students need to ask you a question about something.

Bloomz

Bloomz is a messaging app with several functions. With this tool, you can send updates to parents, as well as reminders about any upcoming activities or events. It also allows you to give the parents samples of the work their children are doing in your online classes.

Class Messenger

Class Messenger puts you in sync with your students and their parents. This tool offers more privacy compared to most of the social network platforms available today. Here, you can create individual or group chat groups for the purpose of communication.

Classloom

Classloom is a free platform for social networking that allows you to communicate with parents easily. Here, you can share important information, news, and messages to the parents. You can even send learning materials through this online platform.

Join Our Class

Join Our Class is a communication portal that parents on-the-go will appreciate. It offers a simple interface where parents can see posts, announcements, photos, and updates that you upload on the portal.

ParentSquare

ParentSquare is a tool that gives you a secure way to communicate with parents about school-related things. You can share your school's calendar, files to reinforce your students' learning, and even communicate with the parents individually.

Remind

Remind is a very useful online communication tool for when you have students from different parts of the world. One of the standout features of this app is its ability to translate messages. This is very helpful when you need to communicate with parents who speak different languages.

Talking Points

Talking Points is another communication app that you can use to send translated messages. As you input your message in English, you can choose a language for the app to translate your message automatically. This helps break down any language barriers for more effective communication.

SchoolMessenger

SchoolMessenger is an online tool that allows you to facilitate the sharing of information between you and the parents. Apart from being a communication app, it offers add-on features that parents may find very useful.

RESOURCES FOR WORKSHEETS

This final set of online tools will provide you with free worksheet resources, which can be extremely helpful if you're in a pinch and you need activities to keep your students busy. Some of these online tools offer free worksheets and activities while others work like an online community where teachers can share their work with each other.

Discovery Ed

Discovery Ed offers a wide range of classroom resources that you can download for free. This is an online community where you can either share or get resources and ideas for teaching.

Education World

Education world is another comprehensive online resource that provides in-depth, high-quality content. Here, you can access over a thousand lessons free of charge.

Jump Start

Jump Start is an online educational tool where you can find fun worksheets and activities for younger learners from kindergarten through the elementary grades.

Scholastic

Scholastic is the best resource option to help awaken your young students' interest in writing and reading. Here, you can get ideas for planning your reading curriculum and even gain access to writing prompts and other helpful resources.

Share My Lesson

Share My Lesson offers more than 420,000 free activities and lesson plans for young learners all the way to high school students. It's easy to find what you need here as the lessons are categorized by topic and grade.

Teacher Education Network (TEN)

Teacher Education Network offers classroom activities and lesson plans that focus on science. This is also an online community where you can interact with other teachers.

Teachers Pay Teachers

Teachers Pay Teachers is one of the most popular worksheet resources for teachers. Here, you can share what you know with other teachers and get paid for it!

WeAreTeachers

WeAreTeachers offers tons of classroom ideas and lesson plans along with free career advice for you, and printable worksheets or activity sheets for your students.

ISL Collective

This site is generally used for teaching English as a second language but with thousands of worksheets, you have a everything from technology and teenagers to World Wildlife Day. There are PowerPoint lessons, video lessons, and the option to complete worksheets online and share them.

6

MAKING THE TRANSITION TO ONLINE TEACHING

You're almost there!

By now, you should already feel more confident about becoming an online teacher. Now, all that is left is to learn how you can transition from a traditional classroom teacher to a teacher who handles virtual or online classes. Having all of the fundamental knowledge you need will make this process easier —and you have just learned this fundamental knowledge.

As an online teacher, you will also have to become a learner. The unique thing about online teaching is that it changes and evolves with the times. Because of this, you have to accept that becoming an online teacher means that you will keep learning new things as you go along. For now, let's go through the basics to help you make that all-important transition into the world of online teaching...

MOVING INTO ONLINE TEACHING

Transitioning into online teaching doesn't have to be a challenge as long as you prepare yourself for what is about to come. Now that you already know what to expect with this modern teaching approach, it's time to get down to business. As you move away from traditional methods or you simply want to add to your teaching skills, you have to make some changes. Although the two have similarities, online teaching is different from teaching in a traditional classroom. Therefore, you can start your transition by preparing the following things:

Adapt Course Materials

If you have been teaching for some time now, then you would already have your own strategies and course materials that you have been using to teach. The good news is that you can also use these for online teaching after making some changes to them. Instead of doing a complete overhaul, why don't you take an inventory of all the course materials you have. After that, check which ones you can modify to fit into online courses.

Now that you understand how online classes and courses are conducted, doing this is much easier. Just make sure that you have a main instructional strategy to use. For instance, will you use a scenario-based instructional strategy or a guided approach? This will depend on the course you are teaching and the age or level of your students. Another way to adapt your course material is by supplementing it with online tools just like the ones we discussed in the previous chapter. This step will take time but it will also make your transition a lot easier.

Create Interactive Lessons

After determining which course materials you can use for online teaching, it's time to take things a step further by creating interactive lessons for your students. As a beginner, this might be too difficult—but don't let that discourage you. Rome wasn't built in a day! Instead, you can use the countless resources available online.

When you have your course outline and the materials you plan to use, make these more interesting by adding interactive elements like videos, games, presentations, and other virtual tools. As time goes by, you can start learning how to make your own interactive activities to ensure that all of your lessons are engaging, relevant, and connected with each other.

Organize and Format Content

The next step is to start organizing your content. After the first two steps, you will already have a lot of materials, lessons, and content that you want to present to your students. But you shouldn't just present these things in random order. Come up with a system for how you will present or share the learning materials.

If you truly want to make things organized, you should also think about the formats of the learning materials you have gathered. Sometimes, using too many formats might be confusing for your students, especially if they are beginners too. Also, some formats are more versatile than others. It would be such a waste if you create content that your students cannot access or understand. Therefore, you have to make sure that your structure and format will provide your students with the best possible learning experience.

Add Assessments

Online teaching involves giving assessments too. Without assessments, it will be very difficult for you to measure your students' learning. After thinking about the materials you will use to teach your students, come up with different ways to assess them too. Online assessments may come in the form of quizzes, tests or even question-and-answer sessions that you can have individually or as a class. If you want to conduct online assessments, you have to learn how these work first. Again, the online tools we discussed in the last chapter will be very helpful for you here.

Invest in a Good Webcam and Sound System

Finally, you should invest in high-quality equipment to ensure that your online classes go smoothly each time. These days, most laptops and computers have built-in webcams. If you plan to buy a new device, make sure to test the webcam and the sound system too. Online classes rely heavily on the video and audio capabilities of your device so make sure that you have only the best. With a reliable device, you can easily transition into online teaching as you won't have to worry about dealing with technical issues all the time.

YOUR GUIDE TO GRADING

As part of your transition into online teaching, establishing a grading system is probably one of the most challenging things you will have to learn. If the company or school you are working for provides you with training to learn a new grading system for online teaching, good for you! But if you are tasked to come up with your own grading system, then you have a long road ahead of you. Fortunately, there are several online gradebooks and grading tools you can use to help you out. Let's take a look at these now:

Online Gradebooks

If you want to use gradebooks to record the progress of your students, here are some of the best options now:

Engrade

Engrade is an online gradebook and so much more. With this, you can record your students' grades while tailoring the evaluation and assessment categories to your own needs. It even comes with a lesson planner and attendance record to help you organize all aspects of your class.

JumpRope

JumpRope helps you embrace a grading system based on standards. With this grading book, you can enjoy quick feedback, convenient assessments, and elaborate reporting. This is a user-friendly tool that you can use to track your students' progress in real time.

LearnBoost

LearnBoost is a free gradebook that you can access online. It has a simple and clean interface making it perfect for beginner online teachers. From signing up to using the actual gradebook, you'll discover that this tool is a breeze to use.

Schoology

Schoology is a social network and LMS that is used by people all over the world. Apart from offering an online gradebook, this tool allows you to develop and share content, apply blended learning strategies, take your students' attendance, and more. Although it's a bit more complex, you can enjoy more features with this tool.

Thinkwave

Thinkwave is an excellent choice for a gradebook tool and it even allows you to communicate the progress of your students to their parents. It's easy to create your account here and from there, you can start learning about online grading.

Online Grading Tools

Apart from online gradebooks, you can also take advantage of other types of online grading tools that offer other features and functions. Some examples of the best ones available now are:

GradeBook Pro

GradeBook Pro offers features like attendance reports, notification emails of status reports sent to parents or students, automatic calculation of grades, and so much more. However, this is exclusively for iOS users.

QuickGrader

QuickGrader is one of the best choices if you're an Android user. This comes with a calculator for you to calculate your students' grades based on their assessment scores. It even comes with an interface that's fully customizable and other powerful grading-related features.

SnapGrades

SnapGrades is another cool grading tool as it offers four options for your online grading needs. You can even use this tool to create seating charts, discipline logs, and to keep track of attendance.

Teacher Aide Pro

Teacher Aide Pro allows you to manage the grades of up to 90 students in each class. With this tool, you can even communicate with your students by sending mass emails or individual text messages.

Viper

Viper is an excellent grading tool if you teach subjects that involve a lot of academic work like dissertations, essays, and coursework. It comes with a built-in plagiarism detector along with a proofreading tool to make checking and grading much easier.

When you think about it, the grading systems of online teaching are a lot like the grading systems of classroom teaching. The only difference is that you can use online tools such as these to automate the process and make it easier. The learning process might be a bit complicated but in the end, learning these online tools and grading systems will make things better for you. Once you have gotten the hang of online grading systems, all you have to do is give your assessments and keep track of your students' progress.

CONCLUSION: YOUR ONLINE TEACHING JOURNEY

Online teaching is a wonderful new approach to teaching that you should learn. Becoming an online teacher doesn't mean that you will be giving up all of the traditional teaching methods you have learned and it won't turn you into a robotic, distant teacher. Instead, you will use those methods that you already know and combine them with everything you have learned in this book to become a well-rounded educator.

As promised, I have shared with you everything you need to know to kick-start your online teaching journey. In this book, you have learned how to become an effective online teacher. If you want to brush up on your teaching skills (mainly the traditional ones) or you want to learn more about blended learning which has been mentioned several times in this book, go ahead and check out the first book in the series that I have written entitled, *Teaching Yourself to Teach*. On the other hand, if you are now interested in becoming the best online teacher and creating your own courses, you can check out the next book in the series that is all about creating online courses of your own. Either way, you will learn even more valuable information to improve your career as a teacher.

Everything you have learned here should have made you understand what online teaching is all about. In the first chapter, we defined online teaching, its benefits and potential downsides, and all of the basic terms you need to understand as an online teacher. In the second chapter, you were introduced to the similarities and differences along with the pros and cons of traditional teaching and online teaching. Next, you discovered the different online courses that you can teach as an online educator. Then, you learned all about the best methods for online teaching—from the basics to the more comprehensive, and practical strategies that you can use as you start teaching online. The next chapter was all about the online tools you should take advantage of to make your teaching experiences easier and more convenient. And in the last chapter, you were introduced to the most practical tips to help you transition into online teaching.

From start to finish, you unlocked a wealth of information to become a skilled online teacher. You are ready for all the jaw dropping, hilarious, outstanding and impactful experiences that come with online teaching. Now that you have all of the information you need, the next step is to use what you have learned. With everything you have learned, you may want other teachers to gain the same enlightenment as you have. To do this, you can leave a review on Amazon to encourage other teachers to take their own steps into the world of online teaching. After leaving your review, all you have to do is start your career as an online teacher. As someone who has been teaching online for some time now, I know that you will have a wonderful time having your own experiences as you discover this innovative teaching approach. Good luck and I hope to encounter you in the digital world!

Thank you for reading my book. If you have enjoyed reading it perhaps you would like to leave a star rating and a review for me on Amazon? It really helps support writers like myself create more books. You can leave a review for me by scanning the QR code below:

Thank you so much.

Selena Watts

REFERENCES

5 Smart Online Parent-Teacher Communication Tools for Keeping Connected. (n.d.). Wabisabi Learning. https://wabisabilearning.com/blogs/technology-integration/best-platforms-parent-teacher-communication

54 Online Teaching Tools To Make Your Life Easier. (n.d.). Jam Campus. https://www.jamcampus.com/best-online-teaching-tools/

Admin. (2011, July 21). *25 Incredible Online Grading Apps That No Teacher Should Live Without » Masters in Education.* Masters in Education. https://www.mastersineducation.com/25-incredible-online-grading-apps-that-no-teacher-should-live-without/

Allain, R. (2020, March 17). *Moving Your Classes Online? Here's How to Make It Work*. Wired. https://www.wired.com/story/how-to-make-online-learning-work/

Asuncion, M. (2019, January 17). *3 Types Of Online Education According To Your Needs*. Edukasyon. https://portal.edukasyon.ph/blog/3-types-of-online-education-according-to-your-needs

Barquero, J. (2019, October 3). *10 Essential Online Teaching Terms*. Computer Aided E-Learning. https://www.cae.net/10-essential-online-teaching-terms/

Best Online Research Tools You've Never Heard Of. (2007, April 10). OEDB. https://oedb.org/ilibrarian/best-online-research-sites/

Bharti, P. (2014, November 3). *6 Great Tools for Blended Learning*. EdTechReview. https://edtechreview.in/news/1624-6-great-tools-for-blended-learning

Blackwell, J. (2019, October 7). *4 Different Types of Online Courses You Can Create*. Jeanine Blackwell. https://jeanineblackwell.com/4-different-types-of-online-courses-you-can-create/

Blecha, B. (2018, May 7). *Teaching with Simulations*. Pedagogy in Action. https://serc.carleton.edu/sp/library/simulations/index.html

Brashear, T. (2018, November 10). *5 Tools To Make eLearning Translation Easy*. ELearning Industry. https://elearningindustry.com/5-tools-to-make-elearning-translation-easy

Bushko, K. (2018, March 20). *10 Popular Edtech Tools for Blended Learning*. Blended Learning Universe. https://www.blendedlearning.org/10-popular-edtech-tools-for-blended-learning/

Caniglia, J. (2019). *Simulation as a Teaching Strategy*. Kent State University. https://www.kent.edu/ctl/simulation-teaching-strategy

Carlos, T., & Libelt, T. (2017, November 24). *The 7 Types of Online Courses that You Need to Know About*. We Create Online Courses. https://wecreateonlinecourses.com/types-of-online-courses/

Chauhan, A. (2018, January 27). *Top 10 Tools For The Digital Classroom*. ELearning Industry. https://elearningindustry.com/tools-for-the-digital-classroom-top-10

Cole, J., & Salcido, A. (2018, September 10). *Best Practices for Teaching Online*. Teach Online. https://teachonline.asu.edu/2018/09/best-practices-for-teaching-online/

Coleman, S. (2010, August 31). *What are the Benefits of Teaching Online?* WorldWideLearn. https://www.

worldwidelearn.com/education-articles/benefits-of-teaching-online.htm

College of Earth and Mineral Sciences. (2016). *Best Practices and Expectations for Online Teaching*. Penn State College of Earth and Mineral Sciences. https://facdev.e-education.psu.edu/teach/bestpractices

CommLab India Bloggers. (2018, March 5). *6 Best Practices of Converting Classroom Training To E-Learning*. CommLab India. https://blog.commlabindia.com/elearning-design/converting-classroom-training-to-elearning-best-practices

Cooper, S. (2016, June 10). *10 Best Practices To Be An Effective Online Teacher*. ELearning Industry. https://elearningindustry.com/effective-online-teaching-obstacles-practices

Darrow, R. (2012, February 24). *What IS Online Teaching and Learning?* California Dreamin' by Rob Darrow. https://robdarrow.wordpress.com/2012/02/24/what-is-online-teaching-and-learning/

Davis, V. (2020, July 27). *Essential Apps for the Physical and Digital Classroom*. Edutopia. https://www.edutopia.org/article/essential-apps-physical-and-digital-classroom

dcmarketing. (2014, July 10). *5 Tips to Adding Gamification to Your Online Course*. DigitalChalk Blog. https://www.

digitalchalk.com/resources/blog/tips-and-tricks/5-tips-adding-gamification-online-course

Dennis, L. (2016, September 13). *Five Types of Online Learning for You and Your Student*. Learning Liftoff. https://www.learningliftoff.com/types-of-online-learning/

Differences Between Online and Classroom Teaching. (2017). Study.Com. https://study.com/articles/Differences_Between_Online_and_Classroom_Teaching.html

Escalona, A. (2016, May 23). *5 Tools for a Better Online Reading Experience*. LifeHack. https://www.lifehack.org/402371/5-tools-for-a-better-online-reading-experience

Gates, B. (n.d.). *Lessons Teachers Learnt*. Lessons Teachers Learnt. Retrieved August 3, 2020, from https://lessonsteacherslearnt.wordpress.com/

Harris, L. (2013, March 29). *10 Of The Best Free Curriculum Resources For Teachers*. TeachThought. https://www.teachthought.com/archived/10-of-the-best-free-curriculum-resources-for-teachers/

Harvard University. (n.d.). *Best Practices: Online Pedagogy*. Teach Remotely. https://teachremotely.harvard.edu/best-practices

Higley, M. (2014, July 8). *Reasons Why Collaborative Online Learning Activities Are Effective*. ELearning Industry. https://

elearningindustry.com/6-online-collaboration-tools-and-strategies-boosting-learning

Holland, B. (2016, September 20). *The Best App for Your Coursework Isn't a Single App.* Edutopia. https://www.edutopia.org/article/best-app-for-your-coursework-isnt-single-app-beth-holland

IGI Global. (n.d.). *What is Web-Based Course.* IGI Global. https://www.igi-global.com/dictionary/web-based-course/32395

Ismail, K. (2018, June 19). *Top 15 Enterprise Video Content Management Systems.* CMSWire. https://www.cmswire.com/customer-experience/top-15-enterprise-video-content-management-systems/

Juviler, J. (2020, July 8). *The 7 Best Video Content Management Systems for 2020.* HubSpot. https://blog.hubspot.com/website/video-content-management

Knerl, L., & Hayes, J. (2020, March 18). *10 Best Distance Learning Tools For Teachers.* Hp. https://store.hp.com/us/en/tech-takes/best-distance-learning-tools-for-teachers

Kovalchik, K. (2013, November 20). *Why Are Introductory Classes Called "101"?* Mental Floss. https://www.mentalfloss.com/article/53734/why-are-introductory-classes-called-101

Kuhlmann, T. (2015, June 30). *3 Reasons Why We Have Interactive E-Learning.* The Rapid E-Learning Blog. https://blogs.

articulate.com/rapid-elearning/3-reasons-why-we-have-interactive-e-learning/

Lawless, C. (2019, January 17). *Blended Learning - What is it and how is it used?* LearnUpon. https://www.learnupon.com/blog/what-is-blended-learning/

Learning Technologies. (2017, March 21). *Web Enhancing Your Course: The What, Why and How of Embracing Blackboard | Learning Technologies.* Learning Technologies. https://www.codlearningtech.org/2017/03/21/web-enhancing-your-course-the-what-why-and-how-of-embracing-blackboard/

Lee, B. (2018, September 13). *Teaching Nomad.* Teaching Nomad. https://www.teachingnomad.com/discover-more/nomad-blog/item/373-pros-cons-teaching-online

Lynch, M. (2017, September 6). *9 Must Have Blended Learning Apps, Tools, and Resources.* The Tech Edvocate. https://www.thetechedvocate.org/must-blended-learning-apps-tools-resources/

Lynch, M. (2018, September 23). *5 Must Have Classroom Management Apps, Tools, and Resources - The Tech Edvocate.* The Tech Edvocate. https://www.thetechedvocate.org/5-must-classroom-management-apps-tools-resources/

Mansaray, S. (2019, November 11). *Web-Based Training for Employees: What, Why, and How?* Your Digital Learning

Expert. https://www.ispringsolutions.com/blog/web-based-training

Matthews, K. (2019, February 1). *6 Apps for Parent-Teacher Communication*. ESchool News. https://www.eschoolnews.com/2019/02/01/6-apps-for-parent-teacher-communication/

Mcdaniel, R. (2013, March 29). *Teaching Demonstrations: Advice and Strategies*. Vanderbilt University. https://cft.vanderbilt.edu/2013/03/teaching-demonstrations-advice-and-strategies/

McIntyre, S., Mirriahi, N., & Bates, T. (n.d.). *Introduction to Online Learning*. Sites.Google.Com. https://sites.google.com/a/hawaii.edu/new-de-faculty-orientation/Step-1

Miller, J. A. (2020, March 20). *Eight Steps for a Smoother Transition to Online Teaching*. Faculty Focus. https://www.facultyfocus.com/articles/online-education/eight-steps-for-a-smoother-transition-to-online-teaching/

Minnesota Online High School, & Minnesota Department of Education. (2015). *What Makes a Successful Online Learner?* Minnesota State CAREERwise. https://careerwise.minnstate.edu/education/successonline.html

Morpus, N. (2017, July 27). *7 Best Free Digital Classroom Management and Collaboration Software*. Capterra. https://blog.capterra.com/the-top-free-digital-classroom-management-software-and-classroom-collaboration-tools/

Mulvahill, E. (2019, January 8). *31 Amazing Sources for Free Teacher Resources.* WeAreTeachers. https://www. weareteachers.com/free-teacher-resources/

Nieves-Whitmore, K. (2020, July 31). *Hybrid Class: What Are They and Are They For You?* College Raptor Blog. https:// www.collegeraptor.com/getting-in/articles/online-colleges/ hybrid-classes-what-are-they-and-how-do-they-work/

Ooi, K. (2020, July 22). *Online teaching vs classroom teaching – which one is better? | Hello Teacher!* Hello Teacher! https:// www.helloteacher.asia/blog/online-teaching-vs-classroom-teaching-which-one-is-better

Pappas, C. (2013, December 16). *The 5 Best Free Gradebook Tools for Teachers.* ELearning Industry. https:// elearningindustry.com/the-5-best-free-gradebook-tools-for-teachers

Pappas, C. (2015, April 18). *eLearning Interactivity: The Ultimate Guide For eLearning Professionals.* ELearning Industry. https://elearningindustry.com/elearning-interactivity-the-ultimate-guide-for-elearning-professionals

Pavlova, I. (2018, July 24). *GraphicMama Blog.* GraphicMama Blog. https://graphicmama.com/blog/digital-tools-for-classroom/

Peachey, N. (2019, May 7). *6 tips for moving your teaching online - How do you adapt your teaching techniques for the virtual classroom?* Oxford TEFL. https://www.oxfordtefl.com/blog/moving-your-teaching-online-how-do-you-adapt-your-teaching-techniques-for-the-virtual-classroom

Penfold, S. (2016, June 2). *3 Simple Ways to Gamify Your Online Learning.* Docebo. https://www.docebo.com/blog/3-simple-ways-gamify-online-learning/

Planetary Transformation Team. (n.d.). *The Transformation Course.* Transformation Team. https://www.transformationteam.net/transformation_course

Podia. (2015, December 16). *Teach Online Like You Teach in Person with These 12 Tools.* Medium. https://blog.withcoach.com/teach-online-like-you-teach-in-person-with-these-12-tools-ca242eeab4cb

Pop, A. (2020, May 19). *6 Reasons to Study an Online Short Course in 2020.* Distance Learning Portal. https://www.distancelearningportal.com/articles/1793/6-reasons-to-study-an-online-short-course-in-2020.html?logout=true

Procter, W. (2019). *Key Differences Between Classroom and Online Learning.* EF Blog. https://www.ef.com/wwen/blog/general/key-differences-classroom-online-learning/

Purdue University Global. (2018, May 15). *Classroom vs. Online Education: Which One Is Better for You?* Purdue Global. https://www.purdueglobal.edu/blog/student-life/classroom-versus-online/

Real Indiana Educators. (2020, June 24). *Is Face-to-Face Communication Essential to Online Learning?* Achieve Virtual Education Academy. https://achievevirtual.org/face-to-face-communication-online-learning/

Renwick, M. (n.d.). *5 Tools for Reading Digital Text.* EdTech. https://edtechmagazine.com/k12/article/2013/07/5-tools-reading-digital-text

Rooheart, J. (2017, April 27). *7 Tools For Your Digital Classroom.* ELearning Industry. https://elearningindustry.com/7-tools-for-your-digital-classroom

Rutka, J. (2020, March 18). *7 Ways for Professors to Transition to Online Teaching During COVID-19.* Top Hat. https://tophat.com/blog/transition-to-online-teaching/

Ryan. (2020, April 20). *Types of Online Learning | Education Program Differences & Categories.* ID Tech. https://www.idtech.com/blog/types-of-online-learning-differences-definitions

S, E. (2020, April 12). *First Steps For Teachers Moving Classes Online.* Mamma Marketing. https://mamma-marketing.com/first-steps-moving-classes-online/

Sabo, R. (2020, July 31). *K-12 & College Educational Technology.* Accredited Schools Online. https://www.accreditedschoolsonline.org/resources/educational-technology/

Sanders, J. (2015, October 30). *7 Necessary EdTech Tools for the Modern Library.* Whooo's Reading. http://blog. whooosreading.org/7-necessary-edtech-tools-for-the-modern-library/

Simon, E. (2018, November 21). *10 Tips for Effective Online Discussions.* EDUCAUSE Review. https://er.educause.edu/blogs/2018/11/10-tips-for-effective-online-discussions

Smith, S. J. (n.d.). *Different Types of Online Classrooms.* Understood. https://www.understood.org/en/school-learning/choosing-starting-school/home-schooling/different-types-of-online-classrooms

Staff Writers. (2016, August 1). *Best Accredited Online Certificate Programs 2020.* Accredited Schools Online. https://www.accreditedschoolsonline.org/online-degrees/certificate/

Staff Writers. (2019, March 1). *The Ultimate MOOC Handbook.* Accredited Schools Online. https://www.accreditedschoolsonline.org/resources/moocs/

Staff Writers. (2020, July 15). *20 Time-Saving Grading Apps That Teachers Love.* Best Colleges Online. https://www.bestcollegesonline.com/blog/20-time-saving-grading-apps-that-teachers-love/

Sull, E. C. (2012a, May 1). *The Online Educator's Complete Guide to Grading Assignments, Part 1.* Faculty Focus. https://

www.facultyfocus.com/articles/online-education/the-online-educators-complete-guide-to-grading-assignments-part-1/

Sull, E. C. (2012b, May 3). *The Online Educator's Complete Guide to Grading Assignments, Part 2.* Faculty Focus. https://www.facultyfocus.com/articles/online-education/the-online-educators-complete-guide-to-grading-assignments-part-2/

Super User. (2011). *What, Why, and How to Implement a Flipped Classroom Model.* Michigan State University. https://omerad.msu.edu/teaching/teaching-strategies/27-teaching/162-what-why-and-how-to-implement-a-flipped-classroom-model

Tamm, S. (2019, December 21). *All 10 Types of E-Learning Explained.* E-Student. https://e-student.org/types-of-e-learning/

TBS Staff. (2016, October 5). *The Best Online Degrees.* The Best Schools. https://thebestschools.org/degrees/best-online-degrees/

Teaching Online vs. the Classroom: A Comparison. (2020, February 26). BridgeTEFL. https://bridge.edu/tefl/blog/teaching-online-vs-classroom/

Thompson, C. (2018, April 5). *6 Tips for a Killer Demo Lesson.* GoAbroad.Com. https://www.goabroad.com/articles/teach-abroad/teaching-demo-lesson-tips

Tomar, D. A. (2018, January 31). *Synchronous Learning vs. Asynchronous Learning in Online Education*. The Best Schools. https://thebestschools.org/magazine/synchronous-vs-asynchronous-education/

Top 10 Online Gradebooks for Teachers. (2015, September 17). ISpring. https://www.ispringsolutions.com/blog/top-10-online-grade-books-for-teachers

UMKC Online. (n.d.). *On the Fence? Five Advantages to Teaching Online*. UMKC Online. Retrieved August 3, 2020, from https://online.umkc.edu/on-the-fence-five-advantages-to-teaching-online/

University of Colorado. (n.d.). *Hybrid Course Design*. University of Colorado Boulder. https://www.colorado.edu/assett/faculty-resources/resources/hybrid-course-design

University of Denver. (n.d.). *Online Teaching and Learning Glossary – Office of Teaching & Learning*. DU. https://otl.du.edu/plan-a-course/teaching-resources/resources-for-teaching-from-a-distance/online-teaching-and-learning-glossary/

University of Illinois. (2020). *Strengths and Weaknesses of Online Learning*. UIS. https://www.uis.edu/ion/resources/tutorials/online-education-overview/strengths-and-weaknesses/

University of Louisiana. (2019, October 1). *Adaptive Learning*. Distance Learning. https://distancelearning.louisiana.edu/teach-online/adaptive-learning

University of Washington. (2012). *Flipping the Classroom*. Center for Teaching and Learning. https://www.washington.edu/teaching/topics/engaging-students-in-learning/flipping-the-classroom/

University of Waterloo. (2012, October 30). *Online Discussions: Tips for Instructors*. Centre for Teaching Excellence. https://uwaterloo.ca/centre-for-teaching-excellence/teaching-resources/teaching-tips/alternatives-lecturing/discussions/online-discussions-tips-for-instructors

University of Waterloo. (2020, April 5). *Synchronous and Asynchronous Online Learning*. Keep Learning. https://uwaterloo.ca/keep-learning/strategies-remote-teaching/synchronous-vs-asynchronous-online-learning

UrbanPro. (2014, January 10). *Top 10 Benefits of Online Teaching*. UrbanPro. https://www.urbanpro.com/online-tutoring/top-10-benefits-online-teaching

Utke, D. (2019, November 11). *Online Teaching vs Classroom Teaching - 7 Surprising Differences*. Teach and GO. https://teachandgo.com/blog/online-teaching-vs-classroom/

Virtual classroom, Online classroom. (n.d.). Timeless Learning Technologies. http://www.timelesslearntech.com/virtual-classroom-explained.php

Vos, L. J. (2014, March 22). *9 Techniques For Online Educators To Gamify Their Digital Classrooms.* ELearning Industry. https://elearningindustry.com/practical-way-to-apply-gamification-in-the-classroom

Vukadin, M. (n.d.). *6 Techniques for Effective Online Communication between Students and Teachers.* Genially Blog. https://blog.genial.ly/en/techniques-online-communication-students-and-teachers/

Wilson, K. (2017, May 30). *Best Practices for Communicating With Students in Online Classes.* Northwestern School of Professional Studies. https://dl.sps.northwestern.edu/blog/2017/05/best-practices-communicating-students-online-classes/

Winstead, S. (2016, March 26). *Top 13 Online Gradebooks to Make Teachers' Life Easier.* My ELearning World. https://myelearningworld.com/top-10-online-gradebooks-to-make-teachers-life-easier/

Zachary, P. (n.d.). *Types of Online Learning.* Fordham University. https://www.fordham.edu/info/24884/online_learning/7897/types_of_online_learning

Printed in Great Britain
by Amazon

59107216R00104